Diamonds in the Coalfields

Diamonds in the Coalfields

21 Remarkable Baseball Players, Managers, and Umpires from Northeast Pennsylvania

WILLIAM C. KASHATUS

McFarland & Company, Inc., Publishers

Jefferson, North Carolina, and London

Library of Congress Cataloguing-in-Publication Data

Kashatus, William C., 1959–
    Diamonds in the coalfields : 21 remarkable baseball players,
managers, and umpires from northeast Pennsylvania / William C.
Kashatus.
        p.   cm.
    Includes bibliographical references and index.
    ISBN 0-7864-1176-7 (softcover binding : 50# alkaline paper) ∞
    1. Baseball players— Pennsylvania — Biography.   2. Baseball —
Pennsylvania — History.   I. Title.
    GV865.A1K39   2002
    796.357'092'27483 — dc21   2001056272
    [B]

British Library cataloguing data are available

Manufactured in the United States of America

Cover photographs: Stanley Coveleski and the coal breaker where he
worked *(National Baseball Hall of Fame Library)*

McFarland & Company, Inc., Publishers
  Box 611, Jefferson, North Carolina 28640
    www.mcfarlandpub.com

For my godparents,
Jane Valaitis and Stan Pawloski,
and my godsons,
Jeremy Kashatus and Billy Kessler

Acknowledgments

Writing a book is a labor of love — not only love for the topic but, in this case, for the people who inspired it. My godparents are two of those people. Jane Valaitis bought me my first baseball glove, bat and cap. Though not a fan of the game, she has always supported me with encouraging words, a sympathetic ear, and unconditional love. Stan Pawloski took me to my very first baseball game. He introduced me to the intangible values of sport, and he shared the story of his dream to become a major league ballplayer with me. For all of these things, I am grateful to both of them.

Just as inspirational are my godsons, Jeremy Kashatus and Billy Kessler. As a youngster, Jeremy was like a kid brother who showed me that I could make a meaningful difference in the life of another human being. In his own way, he inspired me to become a teacher. Billy is like another son, who reminds me of my own childhood passion for sports.

Special thanks are also due to the former major leaguers who are profiled in this book as well as their family and friends, especially Steve Bilko Jr., Norm Brauer, Bob Chylak, Ed Conrad, Edward F. Cove, Harry Dorish, Bob Duliba, Reverend John W. Evans, Pete Gray, Eddie Murphy Jr., Joe Ostrowski, and Alan Sweeney. Without their constructive criticism and support, this book would never have come to fruition.

Although several attempts were made to contact other former major leaguers from the anthracite area who are still living as well as the family members of those who are deceased, my efforts proved fruitless. I regret that the information and insights that they might have provided are not recorded in this book. But their absence makes the assistance of the above-mentioned individuals that much more appreciated.

I am also grateful to the following individuals for their research assistance as well as the permission to reproduce photographs: Robert Janosov, Luzerne County Historical Society; staff of the Heritage Room, Keystone Junior College; and Timothy Wiles and Bill Burdick, National Baseball Hall of Fame Library.

Finally, I am grateful to my wife Jackie, our three sons and my parents, who have always given me their unconditional support and love. Few men ever admit to having heroes, but I am fortunate for having been married and born to mine.

Contents

Introduction

Between 1876 and 1960, nearly 100 northeastern Pennsylvanians played, managed, coached or umpired in the major leagues. Many of them were the sons of immigrant coal miners, who settled in the anthracite region hoping to find the American Dream. They came, initially, from northern and western Europe, and later, from the southern and eastern areas of that continent, especially Russia, Italy, Poland, and Lithuania. Whether they were part of the "old" or "new" immigration though, these hyphenated Americans soon discovered that their "rags-to-riches" aspirations would have to be deferred to the next generation, and only then if their sons were industrious and educated enough to pursue that dream for themselves.

The immigrants became the backbone of labor in this country. Through their efforts, the United States spurred an industrial revolution that lessened its economic dependency on other nations and made it a world power. At the same time, the trials of the anthracite culture — the poor working conditions, low wages and ethnic conflict — resulted in tremendous hardships. Accordingly, they sought refuge in the churches of their own ethnicity, institutions that they brought with them from the old world which would hopefully guide them through the mysteries of the new one. Immigrants established fraternal societies and resided among their own ethnic groups in the small towns that dotted the coal region.

1

Encouraging ambition and personal enterprise among their children, they scrimped and saved to send the most promising of their offspring to college. Motivated by an almost pathologic fear of failure and a refreshing innocence, they believed that self-respect, a good education, and plain, honest, hard work would enable their sons to rise above their humble circumstances and become "somebodies."

Baseball was an important part of the assimilation process. Throughout northeastern Pennsylvania, baseball flourished as a church-sponsored form of recreation and entertainment for coal miners and their families. Nearly every town had an amateur team and some as many as three or four. As the game was embraced by the children of immigrants, it did, indeed, became the national pastime, transcending the various ethnic, social, religious and economic barriers that often divided them from each other. Immigrant coal miners embraced the game and encouraged their sons to play, realizing that for the most talented, professional baseball offered an escape from the difficult times and uncertain futures experienced in the pits. It meant freedom from the most dangerous kind of employment, ethnic discrimination, and fluctuating wages. It was a way to realize the American Dream.

Because of the lack of available statistical and anecdotal information, a comprehensive history of anthracite baseball is not possible without doing serious injustice to some of the remarkable amateur and semi-professional teams that once dominated Pennsylvania's coalfields. Instead, I have limited my examination to the lives of 21 former players, managers and umpires as a representative example of the remarkable talent, dedication, humility and hardship that so many more northeastern Pennsylvanians experienced in their quest to make it to the major leagues.

Of those who succeeded, six are enshrined in the National Baseball Hall of Fame: Christy Mathewson, Factoryville, considered the greatest pitcher of the Dead Ball Era and the ace of the great New York Giants' teams at the turn of the century; Stan Coveleski, Shamokin, who won 216 victories and chalked up 981 strikeouts in a brilliant, 16-year pitching career for the Cleveland Indians, Washington Senators and New York Yankees; Stanley "Bucky" Harris, Pittston, who at the age of 27 led the Washington Senators to their only world championship, becoming the youngest man to lead a major league team to a World Series victory; Hughie Jennings, Pittston, who compiled a .316 batting average over an illustrious 19-year career with Louisville, Baltimore, and Brooklyn before managing the Detroit Tigers to three straight American League championships between 1907 and 1909; Ed Walsh, Plains, who forged a reputation as Chicago's "Iron Man" in 1908 when he won 40 games for the White Sox; and Nestor Chylak, Olyphant, considered to be the nonpareil umpire of the post–World War II era.

Others also made a significant contribution to the game, including Joe Bolinsky (Boley), Mahanoy City, the shortstop of the great Philadelphia Athletics' championship dynasty of 1929–31; Jake Daubert, Shamokin, a two-time National League batting champion with the Brooklyn Dodgers and a steady .300 hitter for 10 years of the Dead Ball Era; John "Buck" Freeman, Wilkes-Barre, who is considered the prototype for Babe Ruth because of his heavy hitting, which carried the Boston Red Sox to two pennants in 1903 and 1904, and victory in the first modern World Series in 1903; Mike Gazella, Olyphant, a member of the fabled 1927 World Champion Yankees' "Murderer's Row"; Pete Wyshner (Gray), Nanticoke, the one-armed wonder who platooned the outfield for the 1945 St. Louis Browns, inspiring a war-weary nation and giving hope to thousands of veterans who returned home from World War II as amputees; John Edward Murphy, Forest City, a .287 hitter who played outfield for the 1913 and 1914 pennant-winning Philadelphia Athletics and later proved to be an honest member of the 1919 Black Sox; Steve O'Neill, Minooka, a star catcher and .300 hitter for Cleveland who played a total of 17 seasons, before managing the Detroit Tigers to the world championship in 1945; John Picus (Quinn), Hazleton, a spitballer who compiled a 247–217 record for eight teams (including three pennant winners) in three major leagues during four different decades, making his final appearance at age 50; Joe "Lefty" Shaute, Peckville, who struck out Babe Ruth more than 30 times in an impressive nine-year career with Cleveland; and Joe Paparella, Eynon, one of the most respected American League umpires in the 1950s and '60s.

Still others enjoyed only brief careers but are, today, considered local heroes in their hometowns, including Steve Bilko, Nanticoke, a power hitter who played with six different clubs; Harry Dorish, Swoyersville, who pitched for the Boston Red Sox and Chicago White Sox in the late forties and early fifties; Bob Duliba, Glen Lyon, who pitched for the Cardinals, Angels, and Athletics in the sixties; Joe "Professor" Ostrowski, West Wyoming, who pitched for the 1951 World Champion Yankees; and Stan Pawloski, Wanamie, a smooth-fielding middle infielder for the 1955 Cleveland Indians.

Based on personal interviews and newspaper and biographical accounts, *Diamonds in the Coal fields* is a composite biography that explores the childhood, adolescent, minor and major league experiences, and post-baseball lives of these 21 men who hailed from Pennsylvania's anthracite coal region. How, for example, did the trials of the anthracite culture inspire their success on the ball diamond? What, if any, values and behaviors did they have in common? How did these shared traits manifest themselves in their minor and major league experiences? How did these players adapt to life after their major league careers came to an end?

These are some of the central questions *Diamonds in the Coalfields* addresses in examining the reciprocal influence of Pennsylvania's anthracite culture and baseball on the lives of 21 men who played, managed or umpired in the major leagues. All of these men played at a time when baseball was truly a sport and loyalty to one team was common. Players wore baggy woolen uniforms, possessed a single-minded desire to be the very best, paid attention to the fans, and performed for little more than a deep and abiding love of the game. They entered a sport that lacked respectability and helped to make it our national pastime. While their experiences speak to a game and its heroes that will never be again, they also offer us something much more valuable than a historical record. They remind us about the power of dreams, the lessons that life teaches in the pursuit of those dreams, and the magic that sometimes occurs when dreams come true.

William C. Kashatus
Lake Silkworth, Pennsylvania
Summer 2000

1

Growing Up in Coal Country

Northeastern Pennsylvania's anthracite region is bounded on the west by the branches of the Susquehanna River, on the east by the Lehigh River, and to the south by the Blue Mountains. At one time this broad swath contained three-quarters of the earth's anthracite coal deposits, providing the entire East Coast with the fuel it needed for consumer heating and industrial production. The area was divided into four coalfields: the Southern Field, located primarily in Schuylkill County; the Western Middle Field, which cut across Northumberland, Columbia and Schuylkill counties; the Eastern Middle Field, at the southern end of Luzerne County; and the Northern Field, which extended from Susquehanna County in the north to Luzerne County in the south.[1]

A monopoly of seven large railroad companies joined by interlocking boards of directors and connected by joint stock ownership to New York and Philadelphia banking interests controlled this region. Their subsidiary mining companies accounted for 70 percent of production and all the employment.[2] In 1880 these four coalfields produced 27,974,532 tons of coal with a total work force of 73,373 men. Three decades later, annual production had nearly tripled to 83,683,994 tons and the total work force was 168,175 men. By 1917, the peak year of production, the four anthracite fields turned out 100,445,299 tons of coal with a total work force of 156,148 men.[3] Coal was king in northeastern Pennsylvania as the black diamond

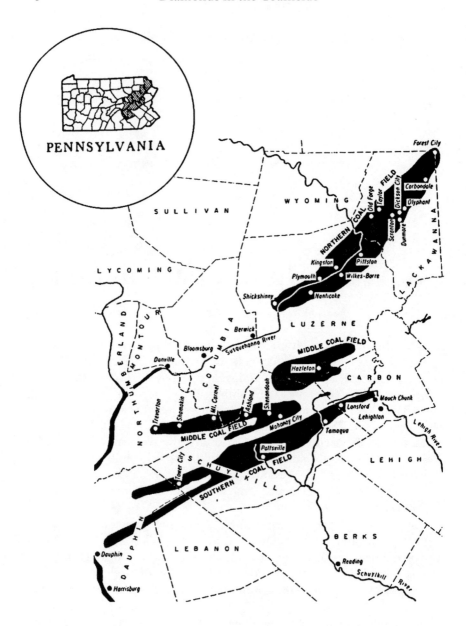

ANTHRACITE FIELDS
OF
PENNSYLVANIA

fueled the factories of the nation's industrial revolution. But the empire came at a terrible price.

The anthracite industry violated a once beautiful valley, leaving mountainous black banks of coal refuse, waste piles of slate and rock, and only scrawny little birch trees to dominate a region once rich in woodland evergreens, oaks and pines. It polluted the sparkling streams and creeks, turning many of them black with coal dust and redolent with the stench of sulfur. Even the Susquehanna River, which once weaved its way through the Wyoming Valley like a silver thread, came to bear a permanent dark tinge, a reminder that the river basin collapsed in the 1950s, flooding out the empty coal beds and destroying whatever anthracite mining still existed.

The coal industry also ignited a fierce labor conflict between immigrants. It pitted the older, more established settlers from northern and western Europe against the newly arrived immigrants from southern and eastern Europe. While the "old immigrants"—primarily English and Welsh in origin—were skilled laborers, foremen, and colliery owners who settled in the coalfields during the early nineteenth century and established the anthracite industry, the "new immigrants" were largely unskilled workers who arrived from Lithuania, Russia, Italy and Poland after the American Civil War. They had been drawn by the lure of the American Dream and a burgeoning anthracite industry that they hoped would serve as their ticket to success. Increasingly, these Eastern Europeans became the backbone of labor in the anthracite region, particularly in the Northern Field. The differences between these two groups were cultural, but they often manifested themselves in the living conditions, working relationships, patterns of mobility, and physical violence that characterized life in northeastern Pennsylvania.[4] There were other human costs as well.

The power of the coal companies was near absolute, being firmly rooted in a medieval-like institution of servitude. Miners and their families lived in poorly constructed company housing negotiated on a day-to-day lease, purchased their goods from company-owned stores, and paid wages arbitrarily calculated not by the hour but by the ton of coal they loaded. The average annual salary was $375, making it impossible for a coal miner to provide for his family. To make ends meet, some miners' wives became the domestic servants of foremen and managers. Working conditions were life threatening. Since even the most minimal safety regulations were often ignored by the company, hundreds of miners suffered severe injury, or lost their lives to cave-ins, runaway mine cars, and unpredictable explosions. Few of those who did survive escaped the dreaded black lung disease, suffering a fate more terrible than death itself.[5]

Growing up under these difficult circumstances presented some special

Aerial view of Glen Lyon, located in the Northern Coalfield. Like many of the small towns that dotted Pennsylvania's anthracite region, Glen Lyon's landscape was dominated by the Susquehanna Coal Company's coal breaker. (Author's collection.)

challenges for youngsters. Children were considered important contributors to the family's income and sent to work as early as possible. Although an 1885 law stipulated that boys had to be at least 12 years of age to work in the coal breakers and 14 to work down in the mines, parents and coal operators circumvented the law by lying about the child's age. In 1903 a new law raised the age to 14 to be employed in the breaker, and 16 in the mines. Since Pennsylvania had no compulsory registration of births, however, these laws meant little in actual practice as a youngster could easily be passed off as "small for twelve."[6] Accordingly, many youngsters became "breaker boys," working in tall, wooden structures where coal was broken and sorted for market. Inside of the breaker was a large room with long iron chutes running from top to bottom. As each coal car emerged from the mine, it was pulled to the top of the breaker by a long steel cable. Once it reached the top, a lever was thrown, the car was tipped and the coal

Before the passage of child labor laws, youngsters were considered important contributors to the family's income and sent to work in the coal breakers of northeastern Pennsylvania. (Courtesy of the Pennsylvania Historical and Museum Commission, Bureau of Archives and History.)

rushed into a shaking machine into the long chutes. Taking their seats on backless pine boards lying astride the chutes, breaker boys would separate the coal from the rock, slate and other refuse as it streamed down, spewing black clouds of coal dust and smoke. To keep from inhaling the dust, the boys wore handkerchiefs and chewed tobacco in order to keep their mouths moist and prevent the dust from going down their throats.[7]

Stan Coveleski, who was born in 1889 at Shamokin, remembers working as a 12-year-old breaker boy at the Luke Fidler Colliery, "from seven in the morning to seven at night, six days a week." For those 72 hours, he received $3.75 or "about 5¢ an hour." "There was nothing strange in those days about a twelve-year-old Polish kid working in the mines for 72 hours a week at a nickel an hour," he insisted. "What was strange was that I ever got out of there. I couldn't play much baseball because I never saw the sunlight. Most of the year I went to work in the dark and came home in the

Stan Coveleski worked as a breaker boy at Shamokin's Luke Fidler Colliery in the Middle Coalfield. Home to 690 workers in 1890, the large breaker is located in the background. (National Baseball Hall of Fame Library, Cooperstown, N.Y.)

dark. Never knew the sun came up any day but Sunday."[8] The youngest of five ball-playing brothers, all of whom worked in the mines, Coveleski vowed "never to look at another mine mule again" when he left the coalfields to play for Cleveland in 1916.[9]

But Coveleski did find a way to hone his pitching skills. Every night when he returned home from work, he would "put a tin can on a log, or tie it to a tree, and stand maybe 40 or 50 feet away and throw stones at it." He continued the practice "every night till it was time to go to bed" and eventually became so good at it that he "could hit one of those cans blindfolded." So good, in fact, that at age 18, the local semi-pro club invited him to pitch for them. "When it came to throwing a baseball, why it was easy to pitch," he reasoned. "After all, the plate's a lot bigger than a tin can to throw at." "Covey," as he was known to his friends, only pitched five games before signing with Lancaster of the Tri-State League and leaving the mines forever.[10]

Joe Bolinsky, who was born in Mahanoy City in 1898, invented a similar method of practice, though he secured his equipment in a questionable manner. Since baseballs and gloves were so hard to come by, the youngster would steal the foul balls from local semi-pro games and stash them away, along with old leather work gloves from the breaker where he picked slate. "I pleaded with my mother and father to buy me a baseball glove," he said. "At first they thought it was a waste of money, but finally they agreed to buy it. My love for baseball was so great, there were times I just threw the ball against a barn door or concrete wall and ran over and fielded it."[11]

Being raised in poverty cultivated a firm resolve to escape a life in the coal mines in any way possible for many of the ballplayers. John Picus, for example, was determined to leave the anthracite region and see the country at an early age. Born on July 5, 1884, in Jeanesville, near Hazleton, he was the son of Polish immigrants who ran a boarding house for coal miners.[12] As a youngster, he attended the local elementary school and did chores around the boarding house, including the laundry. At the age of 12, he became a breaker boy. Despite an elementary-school education, Picus insisted that he "couldn't read or write" at the time, but rather taught himself how to make "letters and numbers" by "copying the characters the mine boss would write on a big blackboard inside the breaker."[13] A year later, Picus joined his father in the mines as a laborer, working an early shift so he could play sandlot baseball in the afternoon. He developed a combative personality early in life, often challenging his stepmother who would not allow him to keep much of the money he earned for fear that he would spend it on chewing tobacco.[14] Picus's mining career ended at age 14 when a fire broke out in the pits. He was working in the lowest shaft and he had to fight his way more than mile through suffocating smoke for a narrow escape. Shortly after, he left home to "ride the rails and see the country," with little more than "a dirty, ragged suit of clothes, a tattered cap, and my own two fists to make my way." When he returned home five years later, he pitched for Connellsville in the Pennsylvania State League and, later, Richmond of the Virginia League. There, he caught the attention of the New York Yankees who signed him in 1909.[15]

"I always had a good arm, developed in stone fights that we used to have as kids," Quinn said, years later when asked about his pitching success in the majors. "Those fights probably helped me to gain control as well as develop the strength I needed to break in as a big league pitcher."[16] Quinn believed that such a rough-and-tumble childhood prepared him to excel at the professional level, unlike others who tried to make the transition from college ball and failed. "I've seen a lot of college players break into the game and snuff out," he said. "They didn't have the sheer bone and muscle that I do. To their way of thinking, baseball was hard work. To me, it always seemed like play, compared to picking slate or swinging a pick in the mines all day."[17]

Ed Walsh, a Hall of Fame pitcher born and raised in the small coal mining town of Plains, near Wilkes-Barre, agreed. After attending the local parochial school for five years, Walsh quit and entered the mines at age 11. There he remained until he was 20 years old, loading coal cars for $1.25 a day. "The hard work I did in the mines developed my body and arms. In the big leagues they called me the 'Workhorse.' I can tell you this, it certainly was a lot easier pitching a game than working in the mines all day."[18]

To be sure, the rigors of mining coal served to develop the strength for which many of northeastern Pennsylvania players were known, especially the pitchers. But the grueling labor also cultivated a fierce independence among some. Hughie Jennings, for example, was an ambitious, likable youngster, but one who occasionally allowed his passion for baseball take precedence over his responsibility to the local colliery. The ninth of twelve children born in 1871 in Pittston, Jennings's family soon moved to Stark's Patch, near Scranton. He was a small, wiry 15-year-old, no more than 90 pounds when he left school to work at the No. 13 Colliery. But Jennings was also an enterprising individual who endeared himself to the miners. Predictably, he was almost immediately promoted to mule driver — the most glorious job of all for a youngster, because it offered danger, excitement, and the freedom to move about the mines.

Often the mule driver was a boy in his early teens, given the responsibility of traveling from one chamber to the next, coupling the full cars together and leaving an empty car to be filled. Because of the narrow passageways, the mules were harnessed in tandem. The smartest mule was chosen as the leader and fitted with a miner's lamp attached to its collar. The driver stood on the front car bumper, using his voice to guide the team. A series of signals gave direction: "gee" meant "right turn"; "wah-haw" for a "left turn"; "whoa" for "stop"; and "giddap" for "go."[19] Jennings developed his own shrill series of war whoops— including "EE-yah!" and "At-a-boy!"— which he would later use as signals from the third-base coaching box during his managerial career. If the mule resisted and refused to move, Hughie would crack his leather snake whip in the air for a warning. Legend has it that he became so adept with the whip that he could extinguish the flame on a lamp without upsetting it.[20]

There were dozens of breaker boys at the Moosic Colliery who were better ballplayers than Jennings, but none with his competitive streak or passion for the game. By the age of 12, he was already playing with the hometown Moosic Pounders as a catcher and without a glove, mask or chest protector. His father allowed him to play until the age of 15 when he was promoted to mule driver. Then, Hughie could only play when his work schedule allowed it. One afternoon he asked permission of the fore-

Breaker boys at work, ca. 1920. For 25¢ per day these boys, not much older than eight, would remove the slate, rock and wood from the anthracite that had been siphoned into various sizes at the top of the breaker. (From the collections of the Wyoming Historical and Geological Society.)

man to be excused to play in a critical game against the Bark Peelers of Minooka, a rival village. After consultation with his father, the foreman denied the request. Undeterred, Jennings left work. His father caught him on the way home and made him put on a dress, saying to him: "If you go, you'll go in that!"

Hughie went to the game anyway, borrowing an extra pair of clothes from his teammates. The following day he was fired by the mine foreman for insubordination and forced to return to his old job as a breaker boy picking slate.[21]

Jake Daubert was also fired by his mine foreman, but for quite a different reason. Daubert, of Shamokin, followed his father and two older brothers into the Blackwood Colliery in 1896 at the age of 11. He was promoted to mule driver two years later. Shortly after, the youngster began pitching for the local Lykens semi-pro club, occasionally filling in at first base. By 1906, Daubert's impressive pitching caught the attention of the mine foreman, who fired him. "You don't work here any more, Jake," he told the young pitching phenom. "With your talent, you belong in the major leagues and I'm going to see to it that you don't work in the mines again." In fact, Daubert somehow managed to return to mule driving that winter, but after making the Interstate League's Kane team in the spring, he never returned again.[22]

Others, like Steve O'Neill of Minooka determined their own fate. Born in 1892 to Irish immigrants who landed in New York in the mid–1880s with five children, O'Neill was the youngest of six ball-playing brothers. Michael, a pitcher, and John, a catcher, would become the first brother battery in major league history, playing for the 1902–03 St. Louis Cardinals. The brothers were known to exchange their signals in Gaelic in order to fool the opposing coaches. Their success inspired younger brother Steve, who by the age of 11 was working as a breaker boy. Three years later he was promoted to mule driver, often working 10 to 12 hours a day.

Since Minooka boys played baseball from St. Patrick's Day, March 17, until the snow forced them indoors, Steve always managed to find time for the game. "In the summers, I asked for an early shift so I could play ball in the late afternoon," he said. "Usually the foreman, a big fan of the local team, allowed me to do that."[23]

Steve won local fame as a catcher for the Minooka Blues, and after his 18th birthday, began pestering his older brother Mike, then manager at Elmira of the International League, for a tryout. "Mike invited me up to Elmira to spend a few days with him during the summer of 1910, and I jumped at the chance," recalled Steve. "I must have been a jinx because both his catchers were out with injuries. There wasn't much left of the season and Mike didn't want to spend any money if necessary so he made me the catcher." Steve caught the next 28 games and impressed a major league scout so much that he was signed by Cleveland the following year, never to return to the mines again."[24]

Regardless of talent, mine foremen and parents tended to indulge the breaker boys and mule drivers when it came to sports, especially baseball. Every colliery, for example, had a blacksmith who was willing to pare down the sturdy branch of a hickory tree into a bat. Foremen looked the other way when their young employees stripped the rubber from bumpers of railroad cars to melt down and use as the core of a homemade baseball. Mothers often provided a knitting needle, yarn, and worn stockings to wrap around the rubber core. When enough material was used to make the proper size, the ball was soaked overnight in water to warp the yarn. After it was dried a knitted cover, with buttonhole stitch, was placed over the yarn and tightened with wrapping twine.[25]

Some of the boys, like Pete Wyshner of Nanticoke, proved to be even more creative. At the age of six, Pete hopped a farmer's wagon, fell off, and caught his right arm in the spokes. The arm was mangled so badly that it had to be amputated above the elbow. Like his two older brothers, he left school after the sixth grade to work at the Truesdale Colliery. Because of his disability, Pete could not work in the breaker and was given the responsibility of carrying a water bucket to thirsty miners. When he wasn't working, the one-armed youngster was teaching himself how to catch, hit and throw a baseball.

"If anything, losing the arm made me more determined to play in the majors," Wyshner recalled. "You have to understand that back in the 1920s, baseball was everything. We played it from morning 'till night. I grew up in Hanover, a small mining village in Nanticoke, and we had a team on every street. There were seven ball diamonds in town. Kids were always playing. So, as a kid, all I ever dreamed about was making the big leagues and playing in Yankee Stadium."[26]

Initially the other kids made Pete a bat boy just to make him feel part of the gang. But he didn't want their sympathy. "I knew that I had a better eye for hitting than most of those kids," he insisted. "I just had to learn how to hit and throw with one arm." Born right-handed, Pete taught himself to use his left hand. For hours each day, he'd walk along the nearby train tracks, throwing a piece of gravel in the air, and hitting it with a long stick. In the process he developed a quick wrist. But hitting was actually the easy part. Learning to field and throw was the more difficult challenge.

"I knew that there was no way I could play the infield because of the quick change of direction and the reaction time that was required to stop a ball to my right," admitted Wyshner. "But if I could find a way to release the ball from my glove quickly after fielding it, I could become a very good outfielder. Eventually I learned that by removing almost all the padding from my glove and wearing it on my fingertips with the little finger purposely extended outside the mitt, that I was able to catch the ball and exchange it to my throwing hand in one swift motion. I'd catch the ball in my glove and stick it under the stub of my right arm. Then I'd squeeze the ball out of my glove with my arm and it would roll across my chest, drop it to my stomach, and into my hand. My small finger prevented it from bouncing away."

By the age of 16, Pete Wyshner was a better player than any youngster in Hanover and most of the adults as well. It wasn't because he had any more ability either. "It was because I respected the game more than they did," he insisted. "I worked damnside harder than anyone else to become a good ball player. I had to. When you only have one arm, you sure don't take anything for granted!"[27]

Stan Coveleski, Joe Bolinsky, John Picus, Ed Walsh, Hughie Jennings, Jake Daubert, Steve O'Neill, and Pete Wyshner were all the sons of new immigrants. They came from large Catholic families where the father and brothers were unskilled mining laborers. That is, they did not have the training of a more experienced coal miner, nor were they certified by the Commonwealth of Pennsylvania to use explosives. That credential distinguished the "skilled" miner from the "unskilled," along with a fairly sizable discrepancy in salary. All seven individuals were forced to leave school at an early age to contribute to their family's income. As they became older they also became more cognizant of their identification with a particular ethic group. Baseball helped to bridge the gap between their new immigrant background and American society. Not only was the game and their ability to play it a way to gain respect among the older, more established families of northeastern Pennsylvania, but also an important vehicle in the assimilation process itself.

Christy Mathewson of Factoryville experienced quite a different childhood, being the son of a more established family. Born on August 12, 1880, in Factoryville, Christopher Mathewson was the son of Gilbert and Minerva Capwell Mathewson. Gilbert was a gentleman farmer, whose ancestors were Rhode Island cotton manufacturers. Journeying west into the hills just south of the towering coal bunkers of Scranton in the early 19th century, these New England migrants intended to establish a textile industry in their northeastern Pennsylvania village and named it "Factoryville." But the machinery they brought with them was never used, the area being too isolated for textile manufacturing. Indeed, coal would become king in the region and Factoryville would never be much more than a tranquil, little hamlet. Minerva, on the other hand, was the daughter of a moneyed pioneer family that placed a high priority on education. Accordingly, the Capwells established the local Keystone Academy, a junior preparatory college, and made sure that Christy and his two younger brothers, Henry and Nicholas, would all attend the school.[28]

The Mathewsons lived in a spacious Victorian house with a winding shallow brook running along one side and an apple orchard on the other. They were God-fearing Baptists who wanted much more for their children than the coal mines could offer, especially for Christy, who they wanted to become a preacher. To secure the proper education for such a calling, the Mathewsons sent their eldest son off to school at an early age and made sure that he continued his studies through secondary school and college.[29] But Christy's passion for baseball threatened to sidetrack those parental aspirations.

Joe Byron, an elementary school classmate, recalls the pandemonium Christy created during their days together in the village's one-room school-

An 11-year-old Christy Mathewson (pictured at center) posed for this 1891 family portrait. His father (far left) was a gentleman farmer in Factoryville and his mother (far right) wanted Christy to become a minister. Instead, he became one of baseball's greatest pitchers. His brother Henry (seated in foreground) also pitched for the New York Giants, though with much less success. (Courtesy of Norman Brauer.)

house. One spring day in 1893 when it was time to take the class picture, Miss Beaton, the teacher, repeatedly "admonished Christy to take the silly, old baseball cap off his head." He appeared to relent and, "boldly striding to the front row, squeezed into place." When all was ready and the photographer was about to snap the picture, Christy "instantly pulled the cherished cap from his pocket, while with the other hand, he wondrously produced a baseball bat." As Miss Beaton "gasped with shock at the sight," the other children "squealed in delight." Christy, clearly pleased with himself, seemed "amused by all the fuss he had created."[30] His experience at Keystone Academy, where he was expected to prepare for college, only increased his love for the game.

"I was still at that age where a country boy is expected to do chores at home, right after school," Mathewson said of his early years at the school. "The Academy building was about half a mile from where I lived, so that when I reached home and finished up my chores, there was no time left to play baseball." So Christy began to skip lunch and stay at school to play ball. If he couldn't persuade a group of boys to stay on for a game, he'd coax one to don a catcher's glove and "spend the whole noon hour pitching to him," trying to master control of his pitches. If he couldn't get anyone to catch him, Christy would go alone to the football field and throw the baseball from one end to the other, in order to build arm strength.[31] All the practice paid off.

Ray Snyder, a boyhood friend who lived in Clark Summit, remembers catching the pitching prodigy. Mathewson gave him two broken fingers and a fractured thumb that never healed properly. "When we played together on local teams, Christy had none of those fancy pitches they use now-a-days," recalled Snyder. "He didn't need them. He had a fast ball that could go through you, a wicked curve that hooked sharply either way, and unbelievable control. And boy, did he love to play! I remember once, in 1895, when we walked a half dozen miles from Factoryville to Mill City to play a game. Christy pitched for two solid hours, striking out everybody at least once. Then he won the game, 19 to 17, on his own hit! We were only 15 years old and we were facing coal miners, some of 'em as old as 21. After the game, we limped home on blistered feet, having earned just a dollar a piece for our efforts."[32]

Mathewson was more modest about his early pitching exploits. "I don't think I was much above the average of the other kids my age in Factoryville," he said. "I just always wanted to pitch and after a while got to be good at it." So good that by the time he was 17, "Husk," as he was known in northeastern Pennsylvania, was a strapping 6'1", 196-pound right-hander with a powerful delivery and exceptional intelligence. He already understood that it wasn't necessary to strike out every batter, or to use his best pitch in situations that didn't demand it. Ironically, Mathewson didn't pitch for Keystone Academy until his senior year when he was elected captain. Until then, he was known primarily as a football player who excelled at fullback and drop kicking. In fact, he even preferred football to baseball, using the latter to earn extra money to get through school during the summer months; something his parents encouraged, though they were better off than most families in the region.[33] Despite his intense passion for sports—or perhaps because of it—Mathewson was offered scholarships to the University of Pennsylvania, Lafayette and Bucknell, where he would star in football, basketball and baseball.[34]

Eddie Murphy of White Mills is the only other player in this study blessed with the advantages that Mathewson enjoyed. Murphy was born in 1891 in Hancock, New York, just over the Pennsylvania border. Shortly after, his father moved to White Mills, near Factoryville, to become a hotel manager along the railroad that ran from Honesdale to Lackawaxen, New York. Murphy grew up playing on the same sandlots as Mathewson and attending the local public schools. Also like Mathewson, he spent his summers earning money by playing for local anthracite league teams. Originally a catcher for Honesdale, Murphy was not quite six feet tall and only 150 pounds. But he was a fleet-footed player and a consistent .300 hitter. John Dorflinger, manager of White Mills, was so impressed with Murphy's abilities that he arranged a baseball scholarship to Villanova University for the youngster, where he eventually caught the attention of Connie Mack, the legendary manager of the Philadelphia Athletics.[35]

Murphy and Mathewson were unique among the northeastern Pennsylvanians who made it to the major leagues prior to 1920. Neither they nor their fathers were forced to labor in the mines and they both enjoyed a higher education. Considering those advantages, their motivation to achieve big league status was largely a personal ambition. Given the lowly status of professional baseball, their decision to become ballplayers was most likely a disappointment to their families as well.

High prices, low wages and poor working conditions influenced the circumstances of the other players and their families. Beginning in the 1860s when the Irish and Welsh worked the mines of the Middle and Southern Coalfields, miners served at the whim of the operators who owned the coal companies as well as the houses, stores and taverns in town. Angered by their lowly circumstances, the miners responded, at various times, by violence through organizations like the Molly Maguires, an Irish fraternal society that destroyed company property, or other groups that formed unions and called general strikes.[36] The most successful of these occurred in 1875 when the Welsh and Irish miners of the Middle and Southern Fields banded together in a Workingman's Benevolent Association and refused to mine for a five-month period. Unfortunately for them, the Eastern European immigrants of the Northern Field continued to work and were able to meet the nationwide demand for hard coal, forcing their anthracite brethren to the south to return to the pits at a 20 percent reduction in wages. Embittered by this turn of events, the Welsh and Irish miners developed a greater animosity toward the Lithuanians, Poles, and Russians of the Northern Coalfield. Two years later when these new immigrants stopped work for three months while demanding a 25 percent increase in wages, the Irish and Welsh miners returned the favor by continuing to work.[37] The struggle between the new immigrant miners of the Northern Field and the Irish and Welsh miners to the south continued until 1900, when, under the dynamic leadership of young John Mitchell, the United Mine Workers Union (UMW) succeeded in organizing all four anthracite fields.[38]

In August of 1900, the UMW called a general strike to protest the arbitrary wage policies of the coal operators. After six weeks, the operators agreed to a 10 percent pay increase in all the fields and the miners returned to work for the first time in their 40-year battle with the owners. This event strengthened the bonds between miners under UMW leadership and made possible an even more successful strike in 1902 in which the UMW was formally recognized as a collective bargaining organization by the mine owners.[39] Nevertheless, ethnic friction continued to dominate the region, especially in the Northern Coalfield.

Nearly two-thirds of the Northern Field's population was foreign born by 1900.[40] For the Lithuanians and Polish who mined that region, the process of social mobility was slow and uneven. It took years for the immigrant laborer who worked alongside an experienced miner to master the knowledge required to pass state certification so he could work independently. Further promotion to the status of mine boss, fire boss or mine foreman was almost impossible for the immigrant. Those were positions that would have to wait for the second generation. Since the recent arrivals were unskilled, they were only eligible for the position of laborer and would not be accepted into union membership. For the owners, they represented a cheap labor force that could be induced into working extra hours in the event of a strike by the UMW. English and Welsh miners, on the other hand, viewed the Lithuanians and Slavs as a serious threat to their own financial prosperity. They were openly vindictive to the new immigrants, intimidating them with both verbal and physical abuse. Beatings, pranks that often resulted in severe injuries, and property damage were common methods employed by the nativist miners.

The first generation of Eastern European immigrants were docile. They didn't want any trouble. Instead they struggled to survive this demeaning treatment, preserving what little personal integrity they could. Their sons, however, refused to tolerate the discrimination.

"When I was growing up in the 1920s and '30s," said Pete Wyshner, "the anthracite industry was in decline. The demand for coal was down across the nation and the Glen Alden Coal Company which operated many of the collieries in the area began to shut down many operations. The Hanover section of Nanticoke, where we lived, felt the effects more severely than many other mining towns. Of the three major collieries in the area, Auchincloss was permanently closed, Bliss was only open for work 150 days of the year, and Truesdale — which had been the life line of our community and the largest employer in the Wyoming Valley — had its work force cut by half and its working schedule limited to 150 days."

"The Slovac and Lithuanian miners created their own union, the United Anthracite Miners of Pennsylvania (UAM), that rebelled against the UMW leadership, who were siding with the owners instead of acting for the welfare of the miners. The UAM demanded a more equal treatment of the miners around here and that Bliss and Truesdale be opened for just as many workdays as some of the other collieries that employed English and Welsh miners. In 1935 the UAM went on strike to force an agreement. When the UMW refused, the state police had to be sent into Hanover to prevent any vandalism. It was like the Molly Maguires around here."[41]

The Glen Alden Coal Company antagonized the UAM membership by replacing them with strikebreakers—many being newly arrived immigrants who were immediately given membership in the UMW. When the UMW miners attempted to travel to work or return home, they were greeted with rocks, gunfire, and abusive language by the striking miners. After a month's time, however, the UAM was forced to concede to the UMW's policy of selective work scheduling, and the strike ended.[42]

Wyshner vividly remembers being chased off the company-owned ball diamond when he and his friends tried to play a pickup game. "The owners were trying to spite us by refusing us the permission to use the ballfield," he recalled. "They realized that many of us had fathers who belonged to the UAM. We had to watch our step because our families depended on Glen Alden for a living.

"I guess when you live under those kind of conditions, you tend to be hungrier than most other ballplayers who come out of different parts of the country. I know I was."[43]

Ongoing labor conflict combined with ethnic tensions, low wages and poor working conditions actually resulted in a better lifestyle for many Lithuanians, Poles, and Russians by the 1940s. Not wanting their children to suffer the same fate, smaller families became more common, and sons were encouraged to attend high school rather than to work in the mines. Not surprisingly, there were several high-school athletes among the ballplayers in this study who were the sons of coal miners but never worked in the pits themselves.

Joe Ostrowski, who was born in 1916 in West Wyoming, was spared from the mines due to an older brother's death. His father was a Polish immigrant who seldom complained about the hardships he endured in the pits, nor did he ever talk much about his work. In 1924, when his eldest son, who was just 17 years old, was killed in a mining accident, the father made a promise to himself never to send any of his remaining four sons into the mines. Instead, Ostrowski contributed to the family's income by working part-time on a farm picking strawberries and tomatoes. Not only was he able to complete elementary school, but he went on to high school where he played both football and basketball. Since there was no baseball team at West Wyoming High School, he learned the game by playing pick-up contests in his neighborhood. "Near the end of my senior year, my parents surprised me by asking if I wanted to go to college," Ostrowski said. "Up until then, I had surmised that I would enter the mines to support our family. Well, I jumped at the opportunity, and enrolled at the University of Scranton. My father managed to put me through by taking out a mortgage on the house. But he kept his promise — not me or any of my other brothers ever worked a day in the mines."[44]

Stan Pawloski, who lived in Wanamie, caught the attention of the Cleveland Indians as a standout shortstop for Newport Township High School. Growing up in the 1940s, Pawloski did not experience the same kind of ethnic discrimination of the earlier generations, but he did learn to "stick with your own kind."

"Back then, there were no formal little leagues," he said. "It was just pickup games until you reached high school. We'd play the kids in our own town. We always felt, for example, that we could beat the kids of the coal-mine bosses who lived in the nicer houses overlooking Wanamie. So we'd schedule games against them. They were 'softer' than us. Of course, there were enough kids on our street to get a team of nine together and play another gang in Wanamie as well. Sometimes we'd get on our bicycles, ride two miles to Glen Lyon and play the kids down there. I guess we met most of those kids in church. Since we were Polish we went to St. Adalberts, the Polish Catholic Church in Glen Lyon."

"Didn't have great equipment. The home team had to furnish the baseballs, and they were always taped up, just like our bats."

"Things were different by the time I got to high school. I played for Newport Township and though we were a small school, we did play the more affluent high schools like Meyers and Coughlin, both of which were in Wilkes-Barre. The ethnic separation wasn't as great either. I talked my Dad into letting me attend church at St. Mary's, the Lithuanian Catholic Church which was just a few blocks away from my home. He agreed once I told him how much more convenient it would be. Of course, the real reason I wanted to go there was because my girlfriend attended mass there!"

Pawloski became a three-sport athlete in high school. But it wasn't easy. His father refused to let him play football, fearing that he would get seriously injured. Instead, the youngster played on the sly. "At first, all I wanted to do was just go to see the games," he recalled. "Since I didn't have the money to pay for admission, I had to find another way to get in. I learned that the school district offered free music lessons to anyone who wanted to play as long as you agreed to join the school band and play at the football games. When I joined the band, I was given a French horn, which was all right with me since you don't have to play any melody on that particular instrument. So I just marched up and down the field, pretending to play! I did that for two years."

By his junior year, Pawloski had established himself as a stellar athlete in both baseball and basketball, and he was getting pressure from fellow athletes as well as the coach to go out for football. Realizing that his father would never sign a waiver form granting him permission to play, he got his older brother to sign it and went out.

"I remember the very first game of the season," he said with a sheepish grin, recalling the ploy years later. "It was against Coaldale, away. As I was leaving the house, my dad asked, 'Where ya' going?'"

...'I'm going to be the student manager for the football team,' I said. 'I'll be doing things like carrying the water bucket.'

"'Oh, good,' said Dad. 'You'll be helping out the team and that way you can also get to see the game.'

Stan Pawloski lettered in football and basketball as well as baseball during his years at Newport Township High School. The day after he graduated in 1949, he signed a professional baseball contract and spent the next seven years playing in the Cleveland Indians' minor league system. (Courtesy of Stan Pawloski.)

"So I go to Coaldale. It's a Friday night, under the lights. Never played a game under the lights before. The field is nothing but dirt and gravel, no grass. I don't remember if we won or lost, but I do remember playing tailback and running as fast as I could —'cause I was afraid of getting tackled on that kind of a field!"

Pawloski had a great game, running for a couple of touchdowns and leading Newport to victory. The next day all the coal miners were raving about his performance in the local taverns. "My Dad went down to the Polish Fraternal Society meeting at one of the tap rooms," he recalled. "One of the miners, who was a Polish immigrant, said to him in broken English: 'Oh, you son, he run like crazy last night! He musta make you proud!' My Dad didn't know what he was talking about. He figured that

I was hustling on to the field with the water bucket whenever there was a time out! But by the second or third game, he figured it all out. I guess he didn't know whether to give me a weapon to protect myself or to be happy for me. I think he kind of enjoyed all the attention he was getting down at the taproom though, so he let me continue to play."

In 1949, his senior year in high school, Pawloski had to make a decision between accepting a football scholarship to the University of Georgia or the University of Pittsburgh and signing with the Cleveland Indians. The prospect of having to carry a full academic course load and devoting nine months out of the year to football seemed impossible to him, so Pawloski signed with the Indians. "I just had more confidence in my baseball ability," he admits. "So the night of my high school graduation, I signed with Cleveland for $4,500. Twenty-four hours later, I played my first professional game for the Stroudsburg Poconos of the North Atlantic League."[45]

Poor working conditions, low wages, and ethnic conflict resulted in a culture of poverty for the coal miners and their families. Such circumstances might have easily led to a general feeling of apathy among the second generation toward their own future prospects. Instead, the trials of the anthracite region only strengthened their resolve to better their own circumstances in life. Coal mining was a negative motivation to succeed and baseball the vehicle for upward mobility. Together with a pathologic fear of failure, those humbling circumstances fostered in the second generation, a keen sense of competition as well as an unyielding desire to be the very best player on the ball diamond. It also cultivated a firm faith in the American Dream, a dream that began on the crude sandlots of northeastern Pennsylvania and, in time, would take them to the green cathedrals of major league baseball.

2

Anthracite Leagues

At the turn of the 20th century and well into the 1940s, Pennsylvania's coal companies promoted baseball for their workers. Operators sponsored clubs, believing that the game encouraged teamwork and offered a healthy release that might otherwise be devoted to labor agitation. Churches of every denomination also tended to sponsor teams, making Sunday afternoon baseball a ritual in the anthracite region.

After morning church services, people would walk home to eat their dinner and then slowly make their way to the nearest diamond to watch two of the local semi-professional teams play ball. Players arrived at about 12:30 P.M. to drag the dirt infield. Pepper games, batting practice, and a quick infield warm-up followed and the game was underway by 2:00 P.M. The contests were often high-scoring affairs. Pitchers didn't bear down until the late innings and only when the score was close. Fans came to see the power hitting, especially home runs. The finer points of defense were usually ignored and errors were common, even on the most talented teams. The hallmark of anthracite baseball, though, was the aggressive play. Sliding into second base with spikes flying high to break up a double play, throwing at a team's best hitters to intimidate them, and barreling over the opposing catcher on a close play at the plate was common.

After the game the players would divide up a keg of beer and boast of their most recent performance. It was a routine, and the most favored routine in the coal region. Hundreds of spectators would fill the bleachers and stand along the foul lines. Playoff games attracted two to three thousand, sometimes more. Since the nearest major league stadiums were Philadelphia's Shibe Park, New York's Yankee Stadium and Brooklyn's Ebbetts Field — all of which were an expensive train ride away — local baseball filled the void.

"In my hometown of Hanover alone there were four teams," recalled Pete Wyshner. "The 'Crescents' were a Slovak team, the 'Hanover Athletic Club' was an English club, St. John's Russian Orthodox Church supported a team and St. Joseph's Catholic Church sponsored the 'Lithuanians,' or 'Lits' for short. Each team belonged to a different league. Since I played for the Lits, I competed in the Luzerne County League, which was one of dozens of associations in the Northern Coalfield at that time. The Lits were more of a family than a ball club. Most of us started playing ball together in grade school. We lived in the same neighborhood and attended the same church."

"When I first began playing for the Lits in 1933, the dues were 25¢ a month. Our season began in early May and usually ended in September because we made the playoffs. Games were played on Sundays after church and our fans would gather along the foul lines to root for us. There would

1934 Hanover Lits Baseball Club, Wyoming Valley League. A 19-year-old Pete Wyshner (top row, fourth from right) was a star outfielder for the team, which was called the "Hanover Lithuanians" or "Lits" for their exclusively Lithuanian Catholic Membership. (Courtesy of Pete Gray.)

be as many as a thousand people at those games. Everyone in town came — mothers with their children would act as soda vendors or ticket sellers, the old-timers who had come over from Europe sat and kibitzed with each other, trying to figure out just what the hell we were doing on the field, and some of the fellas would pass the hat for a donation. It was a social affair, something you just don't see anymore."[1]

Northeastern Pennsylvanians genuinely looked forward to the game on Sunday. For the old men, "greenhorns," who were the earliest of the European immigrants, Sunday baseball was the highlight of their entire week. "Who ve going to play dis noon?" they would ask in broken English. When they were satisfied that their afternoon plans were still intact, they would encourage the younger men of their congregation to "play hart and vin for us because ve going to voot for you gut today!" It wasn't that these old greenhorns loved baseball. In fact, they would spend most of the afternoon along the sidelines playing cards and trying to understand exactly what was happening in the game. Entertainment was only part of it. These immigrants attended the Sunday afternoon baseball game primarily for the same reason they tried to speak English — it helped them to identify their own "Americanness," their sense of belonging to this country. For them, baseball was, indeed, the national pastime because it cut across the ethnic and socioeconomic barriers that often divided them from earlier arrivals and other Eastern European immigrants not of their own ethnicity. They embraced the game and encouraged their sons to play it because they realized that baseball was an important step in the assimilation process.

At the same time, anthracite league baseball showcased some of the region's best talent and served as a social affair where money could be made. Tickets were sold. Bets were taken. Players were paid. In the most highly competitive contests, former minor league players — usually pitchers or power hitters — were hired as "ringers" to help capture a championship. Some were paid as high as $20 a game. At the other end of the spectrum were highly talented adolescents, some as young as 13 or 14 years of age, who were paid a dollar or two for their services. Christy Mathewson, for example, was tapped by the manager of the local Factoryville club at age 14, in the summer of 1895. Being in desperate need of a pitcher to hurl against neighboring rival, Mill City, the manager, a local blacksmith, had heard of the youngster's prowess on the local sandlots. But first, Matty had to prove himself to the other coal miners and farmers on the team.

"Most of the baseball population of the town had gathered to see me try out, which had been well advertised," he recalled. "They lined both sides of the street and watched me pitch. I was putting everything I had on the ball, all the time letting loose all of my speed. It took about two hours' work before they finally concluded that I would do. Afterwards, I got into the big wagon with the rest of the men and started off for the game at Mill City. All the kids with whom I had formerly played stood around and watched me set out. They were naturally jealous. But it certainly was a proud moment for me."

Matty won the game that day, 19 to 17, not with his pitching but with his bat. It was largely a matter of luck, too. "Still batting with my hands crossed, because no one corrected me," he explained, "I happened to swing once where the ball was coming, and I got all my weight into it. The ball sailed over the left fielder's head and the three runners on base came home. Every other time I fanned out."

He continued to pitch for Factoryville that summer, many times having to walk a considerable distance to a game. Win or lose, Matty earned $1 a game, which was "perfectly satisfactory" from his point of view since it was the "first money he had ever earned on a diamond."[2]

Similarly, Joe Bolinsky tried out for the local Mahanoy City team and earned himself a position as a middle infielder. By age 15, he had become the best shortstop in the anthracite leagues of the Northern Coalfield and the best hitter on the Mahanoy club. A year later, he went on to Girardville, a more competitive team, where he earned his first money playing for coal magnate Thomas Kelley, who paid him $2 a game. For that bargain basement price, Bolinsky led the team to a championship and captured the attention of one Philadelphia sportswriter who noted that the youngster had "no loose or idle idea about the game" and "possessed that intangible quality known as class."[3]

Other players were unknown, discovered simply by chance. A 14-year-old Jack Picus, for example, was watching a game from behind a makeshift outfield fence when a ball was hit in his direction. After retrieving it, he threw the ball on one hop back to the catcher, some 400 feet away. The manager of the Pottsville team was so impressed that he convinced the youngster to join his team as a pitcher, offering $5.00 for each victory and $2.50 for a loss. "I figured, 'What the hell?'" said Picus. "I was hungry and without a dollar to my name, so I took him up on it. I pitched for Pottsville and a couple other semi-professional clubs over the next three years before the Yankees signed me."[4]

Hughie Jennings discovered, at an early age, that financial compensation became better as a player advanced to more competitive teams. He learned the lesson so well that he became a tough negotiator when it came time to sign a professional contract. At age 16, Jennings was a 90-pound catcher for Stark's Patch, the mining village near Moosic where he lived. Two years later, he was playing for the Moosic Anthracites, a more competitive club, and making $5 a game every Sunday. There, Jennings

Joe Bolinsky of Mahanoy City was, at age 15, the best defensive shortstop in the anthracite leagues of the Northern Coalfield. He would go on to become a mainstay with the International League Baltimore Orioles and, later, an infield fixture with the Philadelphia Athletics' championship dynasty between 1929 and 1931. (National Baseball Hall of Fame Library, Cooperstown, N.Y.)

captured the attention of Lehighton, an even more competitive team in Carbon County. In 1888, the adolescent agreed to play for Lehighton for $50 a month. Over the next two years, Jennings's fame spread beyond the coal region. Not only could he hit at a .300 clip, but also steal bases and play the infield as well as catch.[5] A career in professional baseball was just around the corner.

During the 1890 season, when Harrisburg's veteran catcher injured his hand, the team's manager immediately signed him to a professional contract. Opportunity knocked again, just a year later when Louisville, then a major league team, stopped in Harrisburg to play an exhibition game. Jennings, who played shortstop that day, went 4 for 4 and made several impressive plays in the field. Jack Chapman, the Louisville manager, purchased his contract immediately after the game. Realizing his worth as well as the value of a dollar, the young ballplayer asked for $250 a month and a $100 advance. Chapman compromised, giving him $200 a month and a $50 advance. Jennings would go on to play shortstop for Louisville for the next three years, compiling a .900 fielding average, and a less impressive .232 batting average.[6]

The anthracite leagues were also a proving ground for professional baseball. Fiercely competitive, the teams received increasing exposure from professional scouts, who came to see the passion with which the miners and their sons played the game. They were not disappointed either, as northeastern Pennsylvania provided some of the finest — and youngest — baseball talent in the country at the turn of the century.

Ed Walsh was one of the most exceptionally skilled players. Originally an outfielder for Plains, he was asked to pitch against a team from Miners Mills when the starter developed a sore arm. Walsh proceeded to strike out 18 of the 19 hitters he faced. "Walsh was an outfielder with the finest arm which I had ever seen," according to Martin Corcoran, the Plains manager. "He liked to give throwing exhibitions from the outfield to the plate and his accuracy was beyond comparison. Those throws were perfect strikes, blazing, rifle-like throws without a bounce. If Ed had continued to be an outfielder, he would no doubt have gone up to the big leagues in that capacity and would be just as sensational an outfielder as any other who ever played the game."[7]

Having achieved local acclaim as both a pitcher and outfielder on a host of sandlot teams in Wilkes-Barre, he was tapped, at age 19, to pitch for an all-star team made up of minor league players. Walsh won the game, 1-0. Word of his success spread outside the anthracite region. The following year he received a telegram from the manager of the Downingtown team of Chester County, requesting that he pitch a July 4 game against their arch rival, West Chester. "Close to 10,000 showed up for that game," recalled Walsh, years later. "I threw nothing but fast balls. I didn't have any other pitch. But I could throw that fast ball for nine innings when I was a kid because the Good Lord blessed me with a strong arm. Gave up two hits, one was a homer. Won the game, though, 4-1."

The following season, in 1902, Walsh joined the professional ranks, pitching for Wilkes-Barre of the Pennsylvania State League. When the league folded, only five games into the season, he signed on with Meriden of the Connecticut State League for $125 a month. Leaving the mines for a better salary, Walsh won 26 games over the next year and a half for Meriden, before he was sold to Newark of the Eastern League. After signing for $1,800, Walsh completed the 1903 season with Newark with a 9-5 record. In the process, he captured the attention of Charles Comiskey, the owner of the Chicago White Sox who signed him to a major league contract the following season.[8]

Other players were recruited by the anthracite teams as teenagers and, shortly after, made it to the professional ranks. Stan Coveleski, for example, was throwing with a friend along the sidelines before the start of a Sunday afternoon contest. Bunker Hills, the semi-pro team from Shamokin, needed a pitcher and recruited the 16-year-old. "I guess those fellows just picked me up and asked me to play because of my accuracy," Coveleski speculated. "Pitched only five games for them and then signed with Lancaster of the Tri-State League. Left the mines forever to play pro ball."[9]

Similarly, Eddie Murphy was discovered when the local Honesdale team's catcher didn't appear for a game. The club's manager, aware of his talent, asked him to put on the "tools of ignorance." Learning of the request, "Big Bill" Steele, a 6'2", 200-pound pitcher hired as a ringer, told the manager: "This kid will never hold me!" Murphy proved him wrong. After the game, Steele went up to the youngster and said: "See you in the big leagues kid!" Three years later, the two met again — Steele as a pitcher for the St. Louis Browns, and Murphy, a catcher for the Philadelphia Athletics.[10]

Buck Freeman debuted with the Wilkes-Barre Amateurs as an outfielder at age 16. The following year, he moved on to the more competitive Spotters where he made his pitching debut. In 1891, just before his 18th birthday, he attracted the attention of the Washington Nationals who came to Wilkes-Barre to play an all-star squad of anthracite leaguers. By the end of the season, the 5'11", 160-pound youngster was playing in the American Association.[11]

For still others, the climb to the majors took a bit longer. But their anthracite league experience proved invaluable as they developed knowledge and skills that would carry them through their major league careers.

Eddie Murphy of Forest City got his big break in the anthracite leagues with Honesdale in 1909. Four years later he was a regular with the Philadelphia Athletics. (Courtesy of Eddie Murphy Jr.)

Christy Mathewson's path to the big leagues was interrupted by his family's insistence that he get a good education. Baseball was a summer pastime that could also be used to earn extra money. During his high school years at Keystone Academy, he pitched for various teams, including Factoryville, Mill City and Scranton. It wasn't until his final year at Keystone, however, that Matty was paid any substantial salary.

SCHULLER   JENKINS   GOLDEN   DUFFY
SCHUERHOLZ   MATTHEWSON N.B.SPENCER-MGR BLANDIN.   BURKE
      TRACY   F.SUYDAM-MASCOT   SCHOONOVER

1898 Honesdale Eagles Baseball Club. An 18-year-old Christy Mathewson (seated in second row, second from left) posted an 8-3 record for the team, while learning the rudiments of the fadeaway—a pitch that would later become his trademark with the New York Giants. (Courtesy of the National Baseball Hall of Fame Library.)

In 1897, he agreed to pitch for the small town of Honesdale for $20 a month and continued the arrangement after completing his first year at Bucknell College the following summer. Posting an 8-3 record that season, he led Honesdale to the league championship. He returned to the team for the '99 season and on July 18 enjoyed one of his finest performances—a 14-6 victory over Port Jervis in which he connected for 5 of the club's 21 hits. It would be his last game in the anthracite leagues, as he accepted a better offer for $90 a month to play for Meridan of the New England League.[12] But his experience in the anthracite leagues taught him how to pitch.

"Honesdale was important to my career," Mathewson admitted, years later when he was the ace pitcher for the New York Giants. "There I learned the rudiments of the fadeaway, a slow curve ball, pitched with the same motion as a fast ball. I learned it by watching a left-handed pitcher named Williams, who could throw a slow out curve to a right-handed batter. Now the natural curve for a left-handed pitcher is the one which breaks inside toward a right-handed hitter. Williams simply exhibited this freak delivery in practice because he didn't have good enough control to risk it in a game."[13]

Williams showed Mathewson how to throw the pitch and the young hurler began experimenting with it. After gaining some confidence, Matty added the fadeaway to his repertoire, mixing it in with his fast ball and a roundhouse curve he had been using. As he made his way through the professional ranks and into the Giants' starting rotation, Mathewson refined the pitch, being able to handcuff a batter with its sudden and sharp drop. The fadeaway made him one of the most effective pitchers of all-time.[14]

While the anthracite leagues attracted the attention of the professional scouting ranks, the players themselves also helped each other to reach the majors. After one of them made it to the big leagues, they looked for ways to gain exposure for talented family members and friends back home. Bucky Harris of Pittston, was given a shot to make the majors in 1916 with the Tigers' organization, compliments of Hughie Jennings, another Pittston native who managed Detroit.[15] Stan Coveleski also credited his older brother Harry Coveleskie, a pitcher for the Phillies, for bringing his talent to the attention of professional scouts.[16] No one, however, did more than the O'Neill brothers for anthracite leaguers in their quest to turn pro. As manager of Elmira of the New York State League, Mickey signed his younger brother Steve as a catcher during the summer of 1910.[17] Eleven years later, Steve returned the favor by bringing pitcher Joe Shaute of Peckville to the attention of the Cleveland organization.[18] Most admirable was the exceptional effort Mickey invested in getting the scouts to take a look at Pete Wyshner, the one-armed wonder.

During the spring of 1943, O'Neill, who had been Gray's manager at Three Rivers of the Canadian-American league the previous year, contacted both minor and major league clubs in the hope of getting Wyshner a tryout.

"No amount of talking helped sell Pete," confessed O'Neill. "I have to admit that I was really discouraged for him. We must have approached a dozen clubs on the East Coast and in the South just looking for a tryout. They'd invite us to camp but never took Pete seriously." O'Neill and Gray went from camp to camp putting on what amounted to a "dog and pony" show. O'Neill would throw batting practice and hit fly balls while Gray put on a demonstration that would astonish the small crowds who gathered to watch their team's annual spring ritual.

"It was really something to see," according to O'Neill. "I'd toss 'em over the plate to Pete and he'd clout 'em to all fields, left, right, center. Then he'd go into the outfield and I'd chase him all over those green cow pastures with fungoes, high, far, and wide. And Pete caught 'em all. I'd marvel at the skill of this lad who'd been — I'd don't like to use the word — crippled. And yet he certainly didn't play like any cripple. He was better than 19 of 20 men his age, weight, and training," insisted the former Canadian pilot. "So there I was with Pete roaming the outfield like Tris Speaker and Joe DiMaggio rolled into one. I'd look around and not a damn person from the club was there to watch him. Absolutely nobody took the trouble to watch him work out. My heart went out to that kid."[19]

O'Neill's perseverance paid off in mid–April when he convinced "Doc" Prothro, manager of the Memphis Chicks of the Southern Association that Wyshner would be a "good risk to take." A week later, the one-armed player received a telegram from Memphis informing him that he had secured a place on the Chicks' roster.[20] As it turned out, Gray's remarkable performance at Memphis in 1944 would prove to be crucial stepping stone to the St. Louis Browns the following year.

Sometimes even personal contacts weren't enough. Realizing that they might be discriminated against in a professional sport largely dominated by the Irish and Germans, some players changed their surnames to get recognized. Those with Slavic, Lithuanian and Polish names either abbreviated or adopted new ones. Often, they were short, quick, and easy-to-remember names for the box scores. "Joseph Bolinsky" became "Joe Boley." "Peter Wyshner" became "Pete Gray." "John Picus," who was frequently chastised as "Pick Ass," adopted the name "Jack Quinn."[21]

What had begun at the turn of the century as a church-related affair or a company-sponsored form of recreation was, by the 1930s, not only a vehicle for ethnic assimilation, but an entertainment industry that generated financial profit and served as a proving ground for professional baseball. The payment of players and charging admission fees, in particular, blurred the distinction between "recreation" and "professional sport," and challenged Pennsylvania's blue laws, which prohibited professional contests on the Sabbath. In 1933 Pennsylvanians were asked to vote on a referendum determining whether the Commonwealth should amend those laws to permit professional sporting contests on the Sabbath. The amendment passed by a vote of 1,546 to 729,220, and anthracite baseball was officially transformed into a semi-professional sport.[22] Much remained the same, though.

The contests continued to be high scoring. Box scores of 9-8, 12-10, and 15-13 games were common. Pitchers allowed the batters to hit, relying on their fielders to retire the side until the late innings of a close game when they bore down. Teams with players in their mid–30s and older committed more errors than those with more balanced rosters. Accordingly, the most talented youngsters continued to be recruited, and paid a pittance of what the more seasoned players earned. Professional scouts also continued to attend the games in order to sign local talent. If anything, they became more aggressive in signing younger players, realizing that they would have to convince their parents that a professional baseball career would, in the long run, be more lucrative than going on to college.

Stan Pawloski began playing in the anthracite leagues at the age of 14. Two years later he was the starting shortstop for the Glen Lyon Condors, one of the finest teams in the Wyoming Valley League. "Zig Najaka, my baseball coach at Newport Township High School was also the Condors' second baseman, and asked me to play shortstop for $5 a game," he admitted. "'Wow!' I thought, 'Five bucks a game!' That was great, just like being in the big leagues. I was being paid to play. I probably shouldn't even be saying this, because you weren't supposed to be paid for playing if you're an amateur, which I was at that time. And here's my high school baseball coach encouraging me to do it!"

"He would pick me up at my home in Wanamie and take me to the games in Glen Lyon. We'd play and, after the game, would hand me my five bucks and I'd head home, feeling like a millionaire!"

While Pawloski spent his summers playing semi-pro ball in Glen Lyon, he starred for Newport's football, basketball and baseball teams during the school year. In 1949 he had to make a decision between accepting a football scholarship to the University of Georgia or the University of Pittsburgh and signing with the Cleveland Indians.

"All of a sudden, I'm starting to feel the pressure," he explained. "Do I play baseball? Do I accept one of the football scholarships? Everyone is getting involved in my life. A physician from Glen Lyon who had connections at Pitt is pushing me to go there. Another fellow from Nanticoke with connections at Georgia is telling me to go there. At the same time, Joe Kelly, a Nanticoke native assigned by the Cleveland Indians to scout me, is hounding me to sign. He wants the $1,000 bonus the organization paid all of its bird dogs if they secured local talent.

"Well, I graduated from high school on a Friday afternoon and here comes Kelly and Mike McNally of the Wilkes-Barre Barons, a Cleveland farm club, offering me a professional contract. I'm only 17 years old and confused about my future. My Dad, God bless him, really didn't know how to help and left the decision to me. So I began to think to myself, 'Gee,

1948 Glen Lyon Condors Baseball Club, Wyoming Valley League Champions. A 17-year-old Stan Pawloski (top row, sixth from right) was recruited by his high school coach Zig Najaka (second row, second from right) to play shortstop for the anthracite league team for $5 a game. (Author's collection.)

I'm not really a great student and I'm going to have to hit the books hard in college. With the kind of football commitment Pitt and Georgia were asking for — a nine-month commitment, which included the regular fall season as well as off-season training — am I going to make it?' At the time, I just had more confidence in my baseball ability than anything else. So that Friday night, after graduation, I signed a Cleveland Indians' contract for $4,500. I learned later that I could have gotten about ten times more. Saturday morning Kelly picked me up and drove me to Stroudsburg where I played my first professional game that same night."[23]

Similarly, Harry Dorish also juggled high school and anthracite league commitments. Dorish, who grew up in Swoyersville, pitched and played shortstop for the Harry E Colliery on Sundays and for his scholastic team during the week. He quickly learned to carry his own weight. "The Harry E players were much older, coal miners," he explained. "Some of them were as old as 35, and they showed no mercy for a teenager. They wanted to win and they didn't care how old you were. But I learned to adjust. The only difficulty I had was during the spring, I couldn't pitch for Harry E because my high school team needed me to throw on Tuesdays and Thursdays. So I ended up playing shortstop on Sundays. But once July rolled around and school was out, I could pitch for the big boys."

Interestingly, Dorish's high school career — not his anthracite league play — attracted interest from the scouts. In 1940 and '41, he pitched

Swoyersville High School to two championships and caught the eye of Joe Reardon, the president of the Scranton Miners of the Eastern League. Six years later, he was pitching for the parent club, the Boston Red Sox.[24]

Like Pawloski and Dorish, Steve Bilko of Nanticoke was also courted by major league scouts, intent on signing him as early as possible. Benny Borgman, of the St. Louis Cardinals, was the most persistent. Borgman saw the 17-year-old Bilko play in an all-star game at Wilkes-Barre's Artillery Park. Impressed with the youngster's power hitting, Borgman knew that he would have to convince the elder Bilko to secure his son's services. Instead of talking to Steve, the Cardinal scout decided to find the prospect's hometown of Honey Pot and follow his performance in the anthracite league. "Any kid who operated out of a place called 'Honey Pot,'" he explained, "was going to be tough for the other scouts to find. So, all summer long I studied the road maps, memorizing every secondary road in that part of Pennsylvania. I watched that kid play in every coal town in the league."

Near the end of the summer Borgman decided the time was ripe to sign his prospect. Sitting out in deep left field on a coal pile, he was watching Bilko perform for the local Honey Pot team when he noticed that three other scouts had discovered his golden boy. Bilko didn't disappoint any of them. He crushed three home runs into left field, one of them nearly knocking Borgman off the coal pile. At the end of the game, the three scouts sprinted over to the youngster trying to get him to sign. Borgman took a different route.

"It didn't take a genius to figure out that the kid was underage," he said. "I drove out to the father's house and we talked about the Cardinals for a few hours. At one in the morning we heard a car door slam and in came the Phillies' scout who had been at the game. The guy took one look at me and the old man hoisting a few beers together, said 'Oh Shit!' and left. The next morning I signed Steve Bilko to a Cardinals contract."

Borgman was convinced that he had signed a future big league star, someone who would one day hit 65 homers. Although Bilko never realized that goal, he did become a feared power hitter in his 10-year career with the Cardinals, Reds, Cubs, Dodgers, Tigers and Angels.[25]

Bilko was only one of many northeastern Pennsylvanians signed by the St. Louis Cardinals. The Cards loved players from the anthracite area because they knew that they could offer a much more appealing future to the strong-armed, raw talent they found in the region than a life spent in the coal mines. That was how they attracted Bob Duliba, one of the impressionable youngsters who signed with them. Raised in Glen Lyon, Duliba lived in the shadow of the great Condors teams. But he was an all-scholastic football player and never had any interest in playing baseball. That is, until his senior year of high school when he took the mound as a favor to coach Zig Najaka.

"My sport was football growing up — not baseball," said Duliba. "I was leaning to go to college on a football scholarship. Never played any kind of organized baseball until I was a senior in high school. Zig, who doubled as Newport's football and baseball coach, kept bugging me to go out because I was a big, strong kid. Then, in 1952, my senior year of high school, he was stuck for a pitcher. The starter was out sick and the others were away on a class trip to Gettysburg. He asked me to help out. I ended up striking out 21 hitters that game. It wasn't because I was a great pitcher either. The damn ball was all over the place. But I was so strong and so fast, everyone was afraid of me. I also lucked out because there happened to be two Cardinals scouts at that game — Bob Kelshner and Bob Breckenridge. They offered me a $4,000 bonus for signing and $175 a month. Since my father died when I was a kid, our family was struggling to get by. So I took the offer. The day after graduation, they put me on a train to Ozark, Alabama, to play Class D ball. I was crying like a baby. Never had been that far away from home in my life."[26]

Other players had to make things happen for themselves. For them, there were no scouts knocking at their doors, no one attending their games, high school or anthracite leagues. They made their own breaks. Joe Ostrowski of West Wyoming played in the anthracite leagues during his summers in high school, first with St. Joseph's Catholic Church in the Holy Name League and later with the Luzerne Croatians in the Independent League. He was a left-handed first baseman who hit for average. No professional organization expressed any interest in him, however, until he went off to the University of Scranton. There he played both college and anthracite league ball.

"You had to create the opportunities for yourself, unless you were an outstanding ballplayer, and I just wasn't a great player," insisted Ostrowski. "I was scouted as a first baseman, but because I wore glasses, one of the scouts suggested that I pitch. He felt that I had a strong arm, and glasses were more common among pitchers than fielders. I took his advice and shopped myself around the local minor league teams as a pitcher, first with the Wilkes-Barre Barons, and then with Scranton, who signed me to a Red Sox contract. Let me tell you something, I was glad that I played those additional years in the anthracite leagues. They were every bit as competitive as the minors and prepared me well for professional baseball."[27]

Similarly, Nestor Chylak and Joe Paparella discovered that their anthracite league experiences were invaluable in preparing them for the challenge of becoming professional umpires. Both men loved baseball but did not have the talent to play at the higher levels of the game. Instead they pursued different paths. Chylak went on to college to study engineering and after serving in World War II, worked in a variety of jobs, none of which seemed to be very appealing. Beginning in 1946, he decided to follow his heart and began officiating at the local semi-pro and high school games near Olyphant, his hometown.[28] Paparella, on the other hand, went to work at the Raymond Colliery in Eynon, where three mining accidents convinced him to pursue his real love. "It was bad enough when a mule kicked Joe in the face," recalled his wife, Josephine, "or when he was trapped in a mine chamber for 12 hours until two in the morning. But when he nearly died from black damp and then was squeezed against a wall by a coal car, that was it. That was all I could take." At age 27, Paparella began looking for work as an umpire at his wife's insistence. "I'd go anywhere at any hour," he admitted. "I did a lot of anthracite league games, high school games, even sandlot games. The pay didn't make a difference. I called games for as little as a dollar. It was the experience that was so valuable. I did that for years until I caught on with the Canadian-American League."[29]

Anthracite league baseball measured the qualities that were most valued among northeastern Pennsylvanians—strength, passion, and endurance. In a society in which the greatest compliment that could be paid to a man was "He's a good worker," the ballplayer who displayed a tough independence and competitive guile quickly earned the respect of others. Baseball also taught self-respect, as the game was one of the few constructive entertainments open to the miners and their sons. Questionable diversions like gambling and the frequenting of brothels were among the limited alternatives in the coal region, where life was short, mean and largely without prospects.

Philadelphia sportswriter James Isaminger, who frequented the anthracite league games, captured best the spirit that inspired the fierce competition of these young men when he wrote: "In northeastern Pennsylvania, baseball and anthracite are synonymous. Those boys who delve into the bowels of the earth to snatch black diamonds from their beds wager all the money they own, too, on the strength of sentiment and conviction. They have no loose or idle idea about the game for the game's sake. They are Irish and want to win, or they are Slavs, Lithuanians and Poles, who have caught the spirit of victory and wage warfare in that enthusiasm."[30]

Essentially then, anthracite baseball was an excellent proving ground for the professional game because it taught independence, pride, and above all, a necessary outlook on life as an incessant struggle where nobody was going to give you anything for free—you had to earn it. That was the attitude these "diamonds in the rough" adopted as they set out from the coalfields to chase after a dream—their dream—to become a major league baseball player.

3

Chasing the Dream

At the turn of the century, baseball was not a reputable profession. Considering it little more than recreation, most respectable people were appalled by the notion that there were those who tried to earn a living by playing a child's game. The sport's poor reputation was reinforced by the constant wrangling that occurred between players and owners, and even among owners themselves. The entrepreneurial designs of player unions and maverick ball clubs challenged owners, who routinely crushed such efforts. Major league owners, in particular, jockeyed to preserve their self-proclaimed position of superiority over the minor leagues as well.

Because of their monopoly of big-city markets, major league owners viewed the minors as wards of their clubs, an inferior but important source for player development. Since an affiliation was necessary, they made agreements to govern the affairs of the minors, only to abandon those same agreements whenever they felt their privileged position was threatened.[1] Consequently, teams were founded and disbanded with great frequency during the early years of professional baseball. Scranton and Wilkes-Barre are examples of this checkered history.

Both of the anthracite towns can trace their minor league history to September 1, 1865, when Scranton's Wyoming Baseball Club and Wilkes-Barre's Susquehanna Baseball Club played each other in the first recorded game of professional baseball in the coal region.[2] Despite repeated attempts

41

by both towns to establish the professional game, baseball continued to operate on an amateur basis. Teams were established as quickly as they would fold, none competing in any organized league until the mid–1880s.[3]

In 1885 the Wilkes-Barre Baseball Club was founded as a member of the new Eastern League, playing a schedule of games against Pennsylvania and New York teams. Known as the "Coal Barons"—a popular name for the magnates of the anthracite industry—the team played mostly on late afternoons and weekends. West Side Park, on the west side of the Susquehanna River, was their home field.[4] The Barons remained a constant fixture in the Wyoming Valley during the next 30 years, though ownership frequently changed and the club played in four different leagues (Eastern, New York, International and Pennsylvania).[5] By 1917, however, a combination of factors led to the disbanding of the league, including poor weather, a declining fan base, and the outbreak of World War I. Wilkes-Barre would not field another professional team until 1923. Scranton experienced greater inconsistency.

Attracted by a group of Scranton businessmen, Dan O'Leary, owner and manager of the New York Metropolitans, transferred his professional ball club to the coal town in May 1886. The new team joined the Pennsylvania State League and played their games at the Sandy Banks grounds off Carbon Street, west of the Lackawanna River. The following year, the team reorganized and joined the International League, a new, 10-team circuit consisting of clubs from Pennsylvania, New York and Ontario, Canada. Scranton competed in the International League for over a decade being used by the major league's Baltimore Orioles as a farm team for player development. In 1898, the team was sold and moved to Rochester, New York.[6] Undaunted by the sale, Scranton's business community sponsored another professional club the following year, entering it in the Atlantic League. The new team was short on talent and tried to make up for it by recruiting former heavyweight boxing champ "Gentleman Jim" Corbett to play first base. After just a season and a half, the team folded and Scranton was left without a pro club until 1904 when John Farrell, president of the New York State League, moved the financially plagued Schenectady team to the anthracite region. Adopting the name "Miners," Scranton struggled during the 1904 and '05 campaigns, but rebounded to capture their first league pennant in 1906. The club experienced mixed success over the next decade under three different owners. When the New York State League was disbanded in 1917, Scranton was, again, without a team.[7]

Despite the political maneuverings and checkered history of the clubs, the minor leagues seemed to capture the interest of Americans during these early years. The spirit of the players and the loyalty of their fans made the minors the true foundation of baseball as the national pastime. Some northeastern Pennsylvanians played for either Wilkes-Barre or Scranton during this early era of the game. Others became local heroes in small towns across the nation. Whether they became Hall of Famers or spent almost their entire careers in relative obscurity, all of the players chased after their dream in the minor leagues and, at least for a time, caught up with it and lived it.

Ed Walsh's first experience with organized ball came in Wilkes-Barre in 1902. He pitched only four games that season before the Pennsylvania State League folded on May 24. The following year Frank Burke, a catcher with Meridan in the Connecticut State League, recommended Walsh to the club's owner. Burke had been a member of the Wilkes-Barre team when Walsh pitched against them as a member of a local amateur all-star squad and was impressed with the youngster. The Meridan owner offered Walsh $125 a month and he accepted.[8]

During his first season with Meridan, the spitballer won 15 games. By July of the next season he had won 11 and then was sold for $1,000 to Newark of the Eastern League. That season he went 9-5 and was drafted by Charles Comiskey of the Chicago White Sox, being given only a small raise from the $1,800-per-year contract he signed with Newark. Though he only spent a total of two years in the minors, Walsh insists that he learned how to pitch during that time. "Early in my career I eased up in the first few innings to save myself, but I found that I couldn't get back into stride after once letting up," he said. "After that, I threw hard all the time. I threw my best to every hitter I faced and found I had the strength to go all the way. But you have to remember that in those early days of the game pitchers didn't have to worry about throwing strikes. We fired away with the idea of getting ahead of the hitter, which is the secret of pitching. Get ahead and then make the hitter swing at your best pitch. When you're behind in the count, you can't afford to try and clip a corner. You've got to get it over."[9]

Buck Freeman also pitched for Wilkes-Barre, back in 1893, after signing with the Washington Nationals. His big break, however, came the following year when he moved up to Haverill, Massachusetts, in the New England League. There he spent the next four years, being switched to the outfield. In 1897 he won the league's batting title with a .390 average in 100 games. Freeman also hit 31 homers and stole 29 bases that year. The following season he was hitting at a .368 clip when Washington called him up to the majors to stay.[10]

Some players would have preferred to remain in the coal region and play for Scranton or Wilkes-Barre. Homebodies like Stan Coveleski and

Buck Freeman of Wilkes-Barre enjoyed pitching in his own hometown after he signed with the Washington Nationals in 1893. He would later become one of the premier sluggers of the Dead Ball Era and a prototype for Babe Ruth. (National Baseball Hall of Fame Library, Cooperstown, N.Y.)

Jake Daubert, both from Shamokin, had a difficult time leaving the anthracite area. "Never forget leaving home for the first time to go play with Lancaster," recalled Coveleski. "It was the first time I ever rode on a train. Had to get a new suit of clothes to go off to the big city, but was too bashful to buy it. So Mom and Dad went to town, picked one out, and brought it home to fit it on me. When I got to Lancaster I was too shy to eat in the hotel with the rest of the team. I'd go to a hot-dog stand and eat by myself instead. Pay for it out of my own pocket."[11]

Instead, Coveleski let his pitching do the talking. During his three seasons in Lancaster he became a fan favorite, compiling a record of 53 wins and 38 losses in 109 appearances. Soon after he was off to Portland where he pitched 64 games in one season, the most by any pitcher in the Pacific Coast League. When asked about his endurance, Covey replied: "I didn't think about strikeouts. The batters knew I had pretty good control and they would often swing at the first pitch. So many times, I didn't throw more than three pitches in one inning." By the time he reached Portland, though, Coveleski had developed quite an effective repertoire, which included a fast ball, curve ball, change-up, and — the pitch for which he is best known — the spitter. "I saw a few pitchers throwing the spitball during my years at Lancaster and started working on that pitch," he explained. "I could make it do practically anything I wanted it to do. At Portland, the spitter became one of my best pitches."[12]

Daubert was just as bashful as Coveleski. A first baseman for Lykens in the anthracite leagues, the youngster, on Labor Day 1906, received an offer to play for Kane of the Inter-State League. Not wanting to leave home, Jake tried to discourage any further interest by sending the club what he

Stan Coveleski was so bashful when he first went to play with Lancaster of the Tri-State League that he'd eat by himself rather than have to sit and talk with teammates over dinner at the team's hotel. (Courtesy National Baseball Hall of Fame Library, Cooperstown, N.Y.)

believed to be an outrageous demand — transportation paid in full and an additional $200 for the remainder of the season. To his surprise, the Kane owner accepted.[13] In 1907, Daubert hit .400 and played a flawless first base for Kane, attracting interest from the Cleveland Indians. The next season, he was invited to spring training with the big-league club. Unable to oust the veteran first baseman George Stovall, Daubert was sent back to the minors. "The year Daubert tried for my job at first, I saw that he'd give me a tough fight," Stovall remembered. "I outdid myself that spring. I hit like a wild man, and in the exhibition series of nine games, I hammered the leather for .750. Jake lost heart. He announced that he didn't have a chance and was going to return home. Cleveland thought the same way and lost one of the greatest first sackers in the game."[14]

But Daubert never quit. Sent to Nashville, Daubert helped lead the team to the Southern Association championship in 1908. The following season he led the league with a .314 average, this time playing for Memphis. Each winter Daubert would return to Shamokin to regroup from the previous season and train for the next one by running along the ice-coated roads in his spikes. His perseverance paid off. In 1910 he caught on with the Brooklyn Dodgers, for whom he would become a regular .300 hitter.[15]

For fans in Buffalo, New York, Bucky Harris was the coal-country boy who shined. He arrived there in 1918 as a middle infielder. Although he only hit .241 that season, his .935 field average and acrobatic style of play quickly endeared him to the fans. The following season he was playing strictly at second base and improved his average to .282.[16] In late August, he gave the hometown faithful a performance they'd never forget in his final game.

"Joe Casey, our catcher, drew me aside while we were playing a doubleheader against Reading," recalled Harris. "He told me that Clark Griffith, the owner of the Washington Nationals, was in the stands. I guess he wanted to put some extra pepper in me." Suffering from a badly bruised finger on his throwing hand, Harris taped the sore finger and the little finger together so he was able to throw the ball better. His concern over his defense, however, allowed him to relax up at the plate and he went 6 for 6.

After the game, George Wiltse, the Buffalo manager, informed the youngster that Griffith wanted to see him. Harris signed with Washington shortly after. "Here's the interesting point," added Bucky. "Wiltse had gotten his job in Buffalo through John McGraw, the famous manager of the New York Giants. They had a gentleman's agreement that the Giants would get first call on any of Buffalo's players who showed major league ability. Wiltse gave me a choice though, between the Giants, Philadelphia Athletics and Washington. Since the A's were down and the Giants already had a fine second baseman in Larry Doyle, I chose Washington. A few years later, after I established myself with the Nationals, McGraw said Wiltse had cost him $100,000 by not keeping the agreement."[17]

In Baltimore, Joe Boley made quite a reputation for himself as the International League's premier shortstop. Boley's rock-solid defense and steady hitting helped to make the Orioles the most successful minor league franchise in history. Starting in 1919, his first year with the club, Baltimore won seven straight International League pennants. The "Philosophical Pole," as he was called by teammates, kept a balanced temperament, win or lose. In the field, he made the hard plays look easy, being equally comfortable going to his left or right. Though his arm wasn't especially strong, Boley made up for it with a quick and accurate release to first base.

During the Orioles dynasty, Boley was a regular .300 hitter, only dropping below that mark once during the seven-year span. His high came in 1923 when he hit .343. Boley was so integral to the club's success that owner Jack Dunn set a $100,000 price tag on him in order to keep major league bidders at bay. Not until 1927 was Connie Mack of the Athletics able to wrest the Mahanoy City native away for $60,000. By that time, the 28-year-old Boley's best years were behind him.[18] Had Dunn sold his contract to a major league club five years earlier, Boley would probably be in the Hall of Fame.

College players were rare in professional baseball during the early era of the game. Most players came right off the farms of the rural heartland or from the factories of the big, industrial cities. Those who did attend college understood that the rules governing amateur athletics prohibited collegiate players from performing for pay. Many collegians circumvented the rule, however, by playing under an assumed name. Others simply left the college ranks to play pro ball.[19] Eddie Murphy was attending Villanova University on Philadelphia's Main Line when he was discovered by Connie Mack of the A's. Mack was the first major league manager to scout the college ranks, believing in the superiority of athletes with an academic background, particularly in baseball which has been called the "thinking man's game." In 1911, Mack convinced Murphy to sign with his club and sent him to Scranton where he quickly proved to be the "whole show." According to the local newspapers, the collegian "played the game to perfection, hitting in the .300 class."[20] From Scranton, Murphy went on to play in the International League with the Baltimore Orioles, where he hit .361 and played right field. He made it to the big leagues with the A's shortly after at the young age of 20.[21]

Similarly, Joe Shaute, who earned a teaching certificate from Mansfield Normal School, was substituting part-time in his hometown of Peckville when a recruiter from Juniata College approached him. Shaute accepted a scholarship to the Pennsylvania college where, in his freshman year, he pitched a three-hit shutout against the University of West Virginia. Charles Hickman, a former Cleveland pitcher and the mayor of Morgantown, West Virginia, attended the game and was so impressed by Shaute's 15 strikeouts that he contacted his former team. The Indians signed the young hurler to a professional contract and shipped him off to the Southern Association where he posted a 7-2 record and an impressive 2.43 ERA with Chattanooga.[22]

Christy Mathewson, however, was the exception, remaining in college while he pitched in the minors. Enrolling at Bucknell in Lewisburg, Pennsylvania, in 1898, Mathewson was the prototype "Big Man on Campus." At 6', 190 pounds, he was a strapping, handsome young man who played the bass horn in the school's band, sang in the glee club and served as the president of the freshman class. He did all this while taking a full course load and lettering in football, basketball, and baseball. An over-achiever by nature, Mathewson quickly earned the respect of the upper classmen, who elected him to both the Phi Gamma Delta fraternity and the Theta Delta Tau, an honorary leadership society for men.[23]

Mathewson was so committed to Bucknell that he wouldn't think of jeopardizing his college career until Dr. Harvey Smith, a Bucknell alumnus, approached him in the spring of 1899 to play pro ball. Smith owned a minor league club at Taunton in the New England League and was in need of a starting pitcher. He persuaded Matty to accept an offer for $90 a month. "The colleges were not so strict about playing summer baseball then, and I needed the money," insisted the young pitching prodigy. "Unfortunately, my experiences with Taunton were anything but pleasant."[24]

Taunton, a small industrial town 30 miles south of Boston, had long been a tail-ender in the New England League. Though Mathewson pitched well against much better teams from Newport, Manchester and Portland, he didn't have much offensive support. Still, he somehow managed to post a 5-2 record in 17 appearances. Worse, Smith reneged on his agreement. None of the players were ever paid, Smith only took care for their board when it came due. On Labor Day the team played a doubleheader at Fall River to raise money for the players' transportation home.[25]

Through it all, Mathewson retained a sense of humor. Writing to a high school friend in Factoryville, the 19-year-old pitcher wryly admitted that his team "makes enough errors of omission and commission to send it to Hades for a prolonged period." One of three pitchers on the team, Mathewson sat on the bench when he wasn't "toeing the rubber." It was just as well. "I pitched in one game," he wrote, "where we had ten errors, beside half a dozen passed balls by the catcher. No wonder we're tail-enders!" Despite "the lack of pay" and "poor baseball," Mathewson concluded he was "having a good time seeing the country."[26]

Mathewson's fortunes turned for the better the following summer when he signed with Norfolk in the Virginia League. There he posted a 20-2 record with 4 shutouts and 128 strikeouts in 22 appearances. The performance attracted the attention of both the Philadelphia Athletics and the New York Giants. "At first I wanted to go to Philadelphia because it was nearer to my home," he confessed. "But after studying the pitching staffs of both clubs, I decided the opportunity in New York was better."[27] Without further consideration, Mathewson left Bucknell after his junior year to embark on a remarkable pitching career with John McGraw's Giants.

At 6', 190 pounds, Christy Mathewson was a strapping, handsome young man during his years at Bucknell College, where he lettered in football, basketball and baseball. (National Baseball Hall of Fame Library, Cooperstown, N.Y.)

From 1925 through 1950, the minor leagues enjoyed their greatest popularity with an era of great teams and leagues that has never been equaled in the history of the game. Public interest in baseball grew dramatically during those years. While the major league competition was restricted to 10 cities in the east and midwest, the minors responded to the public desire for more teams by creating higher classifications for their most successful leagues. The new system resulted in a broad range of teams from Class D, or the lowest of the minor leagues, to Triple A and introduced organized baseball to Americans who had never before seen the professional game. Some of the finest teams in organized baseball played in the high minors at Baltimore, Los Angeles, and Newark. During World War II, the Pacific Coast League and other Triple A leagues had narrowed the distance between themselves and the majors. Instead of incorporating these exceptional leagues as new, competing major leagues, the majors expanded on their own, shifted franchises and used television to raid the growing minor league markets.[28]

Professional baseball also enjoyed a renaissance in the anthracite region. Both Scranton and Wilkes-Barre were awarded franchises in the Class B New York-Pennsylvania League, founded in 1923. Shortly after the circuit was reorganized into the Class A Eastern League, which soon became one of the premier minor leagues in the nation. Eleven Hall of Famers got their start in the Eastern League, including Rabbit Maranville, Heine Manush, Lefty Gomez, Whitey Ford, Bob Lemon, Johnny Mize, and Robin Roberts.[29] During the 1930s and '40s Wilkes-Barre and Scranton became strongholds of the Eastern League. Wilkes-Barre, an affiliate of the Cleveland Indians, played at Artillery Park, a spacious field neighboring the new 109th Field Artillery Armory on the West Side. Considered one of the finest parks in the minors at the time, Artillery quickly became a model for other parks in the league. Pete Gray, who played in Artillery Park when he was with the Elmira Pioneers in 1948, remembers how difficult it was to hit a home run there. "Artillery certainly wasn't a hitter's park," he said. "It was about 345 feet down the lines and with the wind blowing in, it was almost impossible to hit a ball out of there. But it had a great outfield. The grass was like a carpet. You'd also have overflow crowds at those games, sometimes close to 4,000 fans, which was really good for a minor league team."[30] To be sure, Artillery could seat 3,500 spectators and the Barons often played before capacity crowds. When the team captured Eastern League pennants in 1930, '32, '41 and '50, it was not uncommon for them to draw well over 6,000 fans for a single game. In 1927 alone, only their second season playing at Artillery, the Barons drew 147,000 fans for just 68 home games.[31] These were the glory years for Wilkes-Barre.

Scranton, which became a Boston Red Sox affiliate in 1939, was also a showcase for soon-to-be major leaguers, including Eddie Zipay, Mel Parnell, and Jimmy Piersall.[32] Nineteen thirty-nine was a banner year for the Miners, who defeated Wilkes-Barre to clinch the Eastern League's regular season title and went on to defeat Albany for the championship.[33] June's "Booster Night" alone attracted 12,538 fans and several thousand had to be turned away. By the season's end, the Miners drew a record total of 317,249 for the regular season and playoffs and ownership was convinced of the need for a new stadium.[34]

Scranton's new Dunmore Stadium opened on May 5, 1940, and, like Wilkes-Barre's Artillery Park, was considered one of the finest parks in the Eastern circuit. It's magnificent grandstand seated 13,500, and could accommodate a standing room crowd of several thousand more.[35] "Unfortunately, the Miners finished in last place that season," recalled Harry Dorish who was signed that same year by Joe Reardon, the general manager of the club. "But we were loaded with prospects and, in 1946, we were, once again, a contender."[36] By that time, Dorish was pitching at Triple A Louisville, only a season away from Boston's Fenway Park.

The Miner's success was largely due to Reardon's persistence in scouting talent. One of the local discoveries was Joe Ostrowski, a first baseman that the Barons had previously turned away. "Reardon signed me in 1941, and started me at the bottom, in Class D ball," said Ostrowski. "It took me five years to get from Centerville, Maryland, in the Eastern Shore League to the majors with the St. Louis Browns. But if it hadn't been for Reardon's suggestion that I switch from first base to pitcher, I don't know if I'd ever have made it."[37] Ostrowski also remembers the heated rivalry that existed between Wilkes-Barre and Scranton in the 1930s and '40s.

"Of course I had some hard feelings against Wilkes-Barre after they turned me away," he admitted. "After all, the Barons were in my own backyard and I had followed them growing up as a kid. Back then, the local folks would follow their heroes with a deep and abiding affection, moaning when they moved up to the majors. Scranton was the most heated rivalry because they were just over in the next county and, on occasion, would challenge Wilkes-Barre for the Eastern League title."[38] Local newspapers also fueled the rivalry as Mike Bernstein of the Wilkes-Barre *Sunday Independent* and Chic Feldman of the *Scranton Tribune* constantly boasted about the superiority of their town's team.[39]

During this golden era, minor league baseball was more than a game; it was a personal commitment made by the fans on a daily basis in the summertime. Radio brought the games into homes across the region, whether they were played at home or on the road. Claude Haring and Dave Griffiths broadcasted live from Scranton's Dunmore Stadium, and recreated road games, calling the play-by-play off the wire.[40] Thomas Moran did the same for the Barons on WBAX Radio. "I did the play-by-play more or less as a lark," he recalled. "For away games we stayed at home in a cool, lonely studio and went on the air a half hour after the game actually started. We took notes off the wire in cryptic telegraph form. Because of the delay I could make myself awfully good, saying, for example, 'I think so and so might do something.' Of course, that's exactly what he did!"[41]

Special night games honoring players of Polish, Ukranian, Lithuanian and Italian nationalities were popular. Not only did the promotions endear the fans to their local heroes and teams, but they enhanced the already heated rivalry between Wilkes-Barre and Scranton. Predictably, Artillery Park was the scene of some memorable promotions, including a tremendous hitting demonstration by the great Yankee slugger Babe Ruth, who kept a hunting cabin at nearby Blakesly. The Miners brought in Ted Williams, the "Splendid Splinter" of the Boston Red Sox, to do a similar demonstration at Dunmore Stadium in 1940. Not wanting to be outdone by the other, both the Barons and the Miners hosted Max Patkin, the "Clown Prince of Baseball," who thrilled fans with his antics and contortionist movements.[42] And, in 1948, both clubs honored local hero Pete Gray, the "One-Armed Wonder," who was closing out his remarkable career with the Elmira Pioneers.[43]

The post–World War II era witnessed the decline of the minor league baseball. From 1950 to 1965, attendance at games across the nation dropped from almost 42 million to less than 10 million, while the number of leagues fell from 59 to 18.[44] In the anthracite region, as in other small towns across the nation, post-war prosperity and the automobile created a degree of affluence and freedom that separated people from the local community. Youngsters no longer spent their summer afternoons playing baseball like their fathers and grandfathers. Instead, they gravitated to other pastimes, some constructive, others less so. But there were those who still gravitated to baseball and the dream of a professional career.

Bob Duliba of Glen Lyon was signed by the St. Louis Cardinals in 1952 as a pitcher after graduating from Newport Township High School. "When I got down to Class D ball in Ozark, Alabama, I knew nothing about how to pitch," he confessed. "I just wound up and threw the ball as hard as I could. I was blessed with a half decent arm and I could throw the ball with some movement, so they worked with me. I have to admit that the Cardinals were committed to me, too. They had a history of signing Polish players, many from Pennsylvania. When I got there, they had Whitey Kurowski — the old "Gas House Gang" third baseman, who coached me at Peoria — Rip Repulski, Carl Sawatski, and Stan Musial." During the next three years, Duliba gradually climbed through the Cardinals' farm system:

A young Bob Duliba delivers a pitch for Class C St. Joseph's of the Western League where he posted a 12-3 record and a 3.23 ERA (Courtesy of Bob Duliba.)

Class C at St. Joseph, Missouri; Class B at Peoria, Illinois; and Class A at Allentown, Pennsylvania, in the Eastern League. "I was sent back to Peoria, half way through that season at Allentown," said Duliba. "I got hit around pretty good that year and I became so fed up and that I came back home and joined the Marine Corps. That's where I learned to pitch."[45]

After Duliba was discharged in 1959, he resumed his career with the Cardinals. Immediately promoted to St. Louis, he spent the next five years in the majors. Traded to the Red Sox in 1965, Duliba was sent, the following season, to Triple A Vancouver, where he compiled a 7-1 record with 49 strikeouts and an impressive 1.49 ERA in only 44 appearances. In 1967 he was voted the Pacific Coast League's Most Valuable Player, posting a 6-3 record with 37 strikeouts and a 3.18 ERA, before the Oakland A's picked him up to bolster its bullpen.[46]

Steve Bilko was another one of the Pacific Coast League's outstanding players in the 1950s. After an impressive start in the International League with the Rochester Red Wings, where he slammed 34 home runs, Bilko moved up to the majors with the St. Louis Cardinals in 1954. For two seasons he rode the bench before returning to the minors with the old Los Angeles Angels of the PCL where he quickly emerged as the league's most feared slugger. During his three years in the "Palm Tree" division, the Nanticoke native drove in a total of 428 runs and was a consistent .300 hitter. In 1956 alone, Bilko hit .360 with 56 home runs and 164 RBI.[47] *The Sporting News* named him "Minor League Player of the Year," and after the season, the Angels signed him to a new contract for $200,000. At that point, Bilko was among the highest paid first basemen at any level of the game, the others being Stan Musial of the Cardinals and Ted Kluszewski of the Cincinnati Reds. But the lucrative contract came at a price.

Los Angeles president John Holland insisted that Bilko sign a draft waiver, and the young power hitter complied, believing that the no-draft status would not only assure a quick return to the majors, but also a thorough trial. "I signed the waiver because I felt sure if some major league club bought me, it would REALLY be interested in me," he explained. "As for myself, I was positive that if I got that opportunity and could play regularly, I could be of value to any club. But I would have to play regularly. Riding the bench those two seasons in the majors proved that conclusively."[48] As it turned out, the waiver only served to ensure that Bilko remained the property of the Angels. He would play only sporadically in the majors before finishing his pro career, in 1963, again with Rochester, platooning at first base with Luke Easter and Joe Altobelli.[49]

While Bilko's naiveté might have cost him a productive major league career, Stan Pawloski's innocence inadvertently secured him a starting position in the low minors. Pawloski started his pro career in 1949 with the Stroudsburg Poconos of the North Atlantic League, a Class D Cleveland affiliate. He reported to the ballpark the afternoon following his high school graduation. Only 17 years old, the young anthracite leaguer made his way to the locker room, got changed, and went out onto the field to watch the other players take infield. "I noticed that the shortstop didn't miss a single ball, but the third baseman wasn't as good," he recalled. "Of course, I had signed as a shortstop and had my doubts about doing as well as the guy out there. After a while, one of the coaches who was hitting grounders asked me, 'What position you play kid?' Well, I told him third base! Now how stupid can you be?"

"That night, I see my name written into the line-up at third base. Well, I played that night. Didn't do too badly. Lo and behold, I become the team's third baseman that season. To be honest, I really didn't know

Stan Pawloski. (Courtesy of Stan Pawloski.)

much about the position at all. In fact, a few days later, I go into the locker room and one of the players says, 'Hey, kid! Where's your cup?' 'A cup?' I said, 'I don't have any cup.' He asked, 'Where'd you come from?' I told him, 'The coal mines.' 'You must be Polish,' he said, and threw a metal cup at me."[50]

During the next three years, Pawloski climbed steadily through the Cleveland farm system: Class C at Pittsfield, Massachusetts; Class B at Cedar Rapids, Iowa, where he was converted to a second baseman; and Class A at Reading, Pennsylvania, of the Eastern League. At Reading he became a teammate and close friend of Roger Maris, who would go on to play for the Yankees and become the first to break Babe Ruth's single-season home-run record. Pawloski only hit .272 for Reading, but his scrappy defense earned him a .981 fielding average as well as a spot on the Eastern League's All-Star team. At the young age of 22, he was labeled a "can't-miss kid."[51]

In 1954, Pawloski was promoted to Triple A Indianapolis where he split time between second and third base, and hit a solid .280 for a team that captured the American Association title. He returned to Indianapolis the following season as a third baseman. Although his batting average dropped to .267, Pawloski's defense remained rock-solid at .980. "Stan refuses to be benched by an ankle injury that would sideline a less hardy athlete," wrote Gil Sweeney of the *Indianapolis Star*. "Like the old-time ball players who would play with everything broken but their spirit, Stan insists on working the injured joint out rather than let it become stiff through inaction in the dugout."[52] In fact, Pawloski admits that his refusal to take a rest was due more to the fear that he'd lose his position to a younger player than any bravado to play in pain.[53] Still, the majors were just around the corner.

"Like the old-time ball players who would play with everything but their spirits broken," Stan Pawloski proved to be a durable and outstanding defensive prospect with the Indianapolis Indians. Along with Rocky Colavito (standing, seventh from left), Herb Score (standing, sixth from left), and Joe Altobelli (seated, second from right), Pawloski's (standing, fifth from left) .280 batting average and solid .980 fielding percentage helped the Indians capture the 1954 American Association title. (Courtesy of Stan Pawloski.)

Players weren't the only ones to chase after their big-league dreams in the minors. Umpires Nestor Chylak and Joe Paparella also struggled to make their mark. Being older than the players and having families at home made it especially difficult. For Chylak, who began umpiring in the Pony League in 1947, it took eight seasons in the minors to make it to the big leagues where he stayed for 25 seasons. In the early days, he had to be pretty creative to survive. "He would go to the nearest hotel and, pretending he stayed there, go to the men's room, wash up, shave, come out and have a cup of coffee," remembered Sue Chylak, Nestor's widow.[54] During the off-season, Chylak pumped gas at filling stations in Olyphant to add to his income.

Slowly, he climbed the ladder: Class D in the Canadian-American League; Class C in the New England League; Class B in the Eastern League; and Class A in the International League. It was a difficult life. Unlike the players, umpires traveled after each series. They had days off only if the teams did. Their families had to live without seeing them for prolonged periods, eight months of the year. "At first, I resented it because he wasn't around," admits Sue Chylak. "He realized that and offered to do something different for a living. But I knew that Nestor wouldn't have been happy doing anything else. Baseball was his whole life."[55] In fact, Nestor made every effort to be with his family when possible. If he was assigned to a game in Scranton or Wilkes-Barre, near his Dunmore home, he would arrange to see them for a few hours before or after the game. He phoned his family constantly, often inviting them to join him on the road to relieve the loneliness.[56] Paparella was the same way.

He began umpiring in the Canadian-American League in 1938 and advanced to the Eastern circuit in 1940, where he spent the next four years. Although he could have been promoted to the American Association in half that time, Paparella insisted on staying in Class B when his wife, Josie, became sick so he could more easily care for her. "God has been good to me in so many ways," he said of his career years later. "I was an old married man of nearly 10 years and a father when I decided that I had to make a decision between life in the coal mines or something equally as difficult. The more I weighed it, the more certain I was that baseball umpiring should be my future."[57] He credits Joe Reardon, general manager of the Scranton Miners, with getting him his start in the Eastern League by paying him $15 a game to go down to Florida and umpire in spring training. "But mostly, I feel indebted to the old timers who umpired in the Eastern League," he adds. "Men like Charley Moore, Bots Crowley, and Gus Winters encouraged me and explained what to expect when I reached the higher levels and how to handle each situation. Associating with these charitable and knowledgeable men was the turning point for me."[58]

During the 1950s, when New York's Yankee Stadium, Brooklyn's Ebbets Field, and Philadelphia's Shibe Park were only a car ride away for northeastern Pennsylvanians, Wilkes-Barre's Artillery Park and Scranton's Dunmore Stadium became increasingly distant. Like those small beloved ballparks, minor league baseball in the anthracite region went into decline. Scranton peaked in 1946 when the Miners won the pennant by 18 games. Afterwards, the team witnessed a gradual drop in attendance, finally folding in 1953 while under control of the Washington Senators. Lacking a tenant, Dunmore Stadium was dismantled and freighted in sections to Richmond, Virginia, where it would serve as home to that city's minor league teams for the next two decades.[59] Wilkes-Barre experienced a similar fate.

After World War II, attendance began to decline and Cleveland transferred its franchise to Reading in 1951, in spite of the fact that the Barons had captured another Eastern League championship. A new Wilkes-Barre team developed a working agreement with the Detroit Tigers, but even they withdrew their sponsorship after the '54 season, again, after the Barons clinched the championship. Attempting to operate as an independent club in 1955, the Barons folded midway through the season as the Eastern

League transferred the franchise to Johnstown, Pennsylvania.[60] A rich history of colorful players and memorable games had come to an end. The anthracite region would not see professional baseball again until 1989 when the Scranton/Wilkes-Barre Red Barons were established, their name a legacy of two great minor league teams that once dominated northeastern Pennsylvania.

4

Serving Uncle Sam

Baseball's image as the national pastime has been sorely tested whenever the United States has gone to war. The popularity of the sport as well as the profit motive of the owners often raised questions about whether baseball was an "essential employment." Players, too, were forced to choose between competing loyalties to country and career. For some of northeastern Pennsylvania's ballplayers, Uncle Sam postponed the journey to the big leagues. Others were ushered into special services and permitted to play ball for the various branches of the military. Still other pursued their careers uninterrupted and, in one case, wartime offered an opportunity to crack the majors while the established stars were serving their country abroad.

When America entered World War I in April 1917, the baseball season was already underway. While the United States mobilized to put five million men in uniform, two million of which would be heading to the battlefront in France, major league owners pressed on with business as usual, hoping that the game would be protected by the government for its morale-boosting potential.[1] To show their support for the war effort, clubs established bat and ball funds for soldiers, admitted servicemen free of charge, sported flags on uniform sleeves, and sponsored patriotic pregame shows.[2] Concerned about the retention of their teams, however, owners ordered players to remain with the club, even if it made them easier to draft. Worse, the lack of voluntary enlistments and the players' demand for higher salaries hurt baseball's image.[3] Increasingly, ballplayers were criticized by the fans for their reluctance to join up with thousands of young Americans, known as "doughboys" to the admiring public.

In late May 1918, Provost Marshall General Enoch Crowder put the matter to rest when he issued a "work-or-fight" order, forcing all draft age men either to enter the military or essential industries by July 1. Shortly after, Secretary of War Newton Baker restricted the 1918 season to 130 games, some 24 less than the regular schedule. The season was to end on September 2, with a grace period for the World Series. Baseball was ruled "non-essential," despite the pleas from owners to keep the sport going without modification. Before the July deadline many players and managers were drafted, or left their teams. In all, over 255 major leaguers went into the armed forces.[4] Among those to serve were Joe Boley, Mike Gazella and Christy Mathewson.

Because World War I veterans refused to discuss their memories of war, nothing is known of Boley's wartime experience and very little about Gazella's or Mathewson's. What is known about Gazella is that his anthracite league career with Olyphant was interrupted by voluntary enlistment. Only 22 years old, he joined an artillery unit and was shipped to France where he saw considerable action. There, he suffered poisoning from exposure to mustard gas and was honorably discharged shortly after.[5]

Matty, who was then managing the Cincinnati Reds, did not have to join up. He was 37 years old at the time, well past the 31-year-old cutoff the Selective Service Act established. Nor was his decision based on a desire for personal recognition. When he enlisted in August 1918, there was no way of predicting how much longer the war would continue. Germany refused to admit defeat, despite the enormous losses it had already suffered and the tremendous influx of U.S. support to France and Britain. In fact, the Germans were, at the time, preparing for a massive attack at Meuse-Argonne in northeast France, which would prove to be the watershed battle of the war. Thus, Mathewson's decision to serve was not influenced by either public opinion or feelings of guilt, but rather a genuine desire to serve his country.[6]

Like other baseball luminaries who were too old for military service, Matty joined the Chemical Warfare Service (CWS) and was assigned to train inexperienced doughboys how to fight against the poisonous mustard gas used by Germany.[7] Given accelerated training as well as the commission of a captain, Mathewson was made an instructor in the Gas and Flame Division of CWS and shipped out to Chaumont, France, near the Belgian border. Sometime over the next three months he was exposed to mustard gas on at least two occasions: once during a training exercise in an airtight chamber used to simulate battlefield conditions and again while

Captain Christy Mathewson joined the Chemical Warefare Service during World War I and instructed inexperienced doughboys in gas warfare in France. Exposed to the poisonous mustard gas, Mathewson's health rapidly deteriorated after the war. He died at the young age of 45. (National Baseball Hall of Fame Library, Cooperstown, N.Y.)

examining ammunition dumps left behind by Germans. Already weakened by the flu, which he contracted during the voyage to France, Matty may have been more vulnerable to the gas fumes during these instances. As a result of the exposure, he was hospitalized in France before and after the long-awaited armistice, which finally came on November 11, 1918.[8]

Baseball responded more quickly and effectively during World War II, most likely due to the image problems it suffered two decades earlier. Shortly after the attack on Pearl Harbor on December 7, 1941, players began to enlist in record numbers. The exodus of first-class players, along with the concern that transporting the 16 major league clubs around the country would divert natural resources necessary for the war effort, led Baseball Commissioner Kenesaw Mountain Landis to consider suspending major league play during the war. Reluctant to begin the 1942 season only to have it disbanded, Landis wrote to President Franklin D. Roosevelt seeking advice. "Baseball is about to adopt schedules, sign players, make vast commitments, and go to training camps," he informed the president. "What do you want it to do? If you believe we ought to close down for the duration of the war, we are ready to do so immediately, if you feel we ought to continue, we would be delighted to do so. We await your order."[9]

The president's response was immediate and encouraging. He believed it imperative to continue major league play, something he considered essential to national morale. "I honestly feel that it would be best for the country to keep baseball going," he wrote. "There will be fewer people unemployed and everybody will work longer hours and harder than ever before. And that means that they ought to have a chance for recreation and for taking their minds off work even more than before."

Roosevelt's "green light," however, came with the strongly worded suggestions to extend night games "because it gives an opportunity to the day shift to see a game occasionally," and to persuade all those players who were physically capable to enlist in the armed services. "As to the players themselves," wrote Roosevelt, "I know you agree with me that individual players who are of active military or naval age should go, without question, into the services. Even if the actual quality of the teams is lowered by the greater use of older players, this will not dampen the popularity of the sport."[10]

FDR's directive only reinforced what had already become government policy under the Selective Service Act passed by Congress during the pre-war preparations of 1940. According to this act, men 18 through 45 years of age were required to register but only those between the ages of 20 and 32 would actually be called to serve. The act was revised by Congress in November 1921, allowing for the conscription of men 18 and 19 years of age. Draft deferments were to be based on the number of dependents a man had and the extent to which his civilian job contributed to the war effort. Single men with no dependents were the first to be drafted. Second to go were single men with "collateral" dependents such as parents but without a job that contributed to the war effort. Third were single men with collateral dependents and with a job that did contribute. Fourth in the hierarchy were married men without children but without a contributing job. Fifth were those men who were married without children but with a contributing job. Sixth were married men with children but without a contributing job. And seventh were married men with children and with a job that contributed to the war effort.

Although local draft boards determined which jobs were essential to the war effort and standards varied from community to community, as did the number of men available to meet the local draft quotas, those jobs considered "essential" generally included: farmers, firemen, physicians, state legislators, teachers and coal miners.[11] In fact, World War II, resuscitated a declining coal industry in northeastern Pennsylvania.

Anthracite mines were working at 100 percent capacity by the summer of '42 as the supply of coal could not meet the demand. Glen Alden, the largest coal company in the anthracite region, was producing an average of 50,000 tons a day at its collieries in Luzerne and Lackawanna Counties and still suffered from a serious labor shortage. Many mine workers had either entered the military or had relocated to other states in search of employment prior to the war. Now the coal operators scrambled to find workers, appealing to those from the less productive anthracite fields to the south. Something more had to be done, though. Arguing that petroleum was simply not plentiful enough to satisfy national fuel needs, Thomas Kennedy, Secretary-Treasurer of the United Mine Workers of America and a member of the War Labor Board, persuaded Selective Service to exempt "needed" mine workers from the draft.[12]

Of course, "professional baseball player" was not considered an essential employment, at least initially. Among the 12 million Americans who went to war during the period from 1942 to 1945, there were 500 major league baseball players and nearly 4,000 minor leaguers. The majority of these men enlisted, refusing to accept any special treatment because of their personal circumstances.[13] Joe Ostrowski, a hot young pitching prospect in the Red Sox organization, went 21-8 for Greensboro in the Piedmont League in1942. Slated for promotion to Louisville of the American Association, he joined the Air Force instead. Ostrowski was out of the game for the next three years. Nineteen of those months were spent in Italy, though he never saw any fighting.[14] Similarly, Harry Dorish, another one of Boston's young pitching prospects, left the Scranton Miners in 1943 to join the Army. He served on Guadalcanal as a platoon sergeant before returning to pro ball in 1946.[15]

Sgt. Harry Dorish displays his winning pitching form to a fellow officer on Guadalcanal in October of 1944. (Courtesy of Mrs. Harry Dorish.)

Umpire Nestor Chylak also enlisted and quickly earned respect for his leadership abilities. Named a platoon sergeant in the 424th Infantry Regiment, he was struck by shrapnel from an exploding German shell in January 1945 and almost lost his eyesight. After an 8-week stay in the hospital, he was decorated with both the silver star and purple heart and honorably discharged.[16] Joe Paparella, on the other hand, was allowed to continue his umpiring career. Being married with children, he qualified for a lower draft number, but a full deferment came when FDR absented males over age 31 engaged in the entertainment business.[17]

Pete Gray's case was the most exceptional. He was more than willing to put his professional career on hold for the war effort, trying to enlist shortly after Pearl Harbor. But the local draft board refused to take him because of the missing right arm. Classified 4-F, physically unfit for military service, Gray spent the war at home. "I never deserved the 4-F classification," he said bitterly, recalling the experience years later. "If I could teach myself to play baseball with one arm, I sure as hell could handle a rifle or anything else the military threw my way!"[18] In fact, the 4-F status turned out to be a blessing in disguise.

Because the war stripped the major leagues of some of its finest talent, clubs were forced to search for 4-Fs like Gray, who had been struggling his way up the "baseball ladder" from semipro to Double A ball for nearly a decade. Not only did the war offer Gray the opportunity to crack the majors, but it also made him a national hero. Signed by the Memphis Chicks of the Southern Association in 1943, Gray captured the national spotlight by collecting 131 hits, 42 RBI, and hitting .289. The following year *The Sporting News* named him the league's Most Valuable Player for his .333 average, 60 RBI and 68 stolen bases.[19] After the season the St. Louis Browns purchased Gray's contract for $20,000, the largest sum of money spent on a Southern Association player to that date.[20] More important, the "One-Armed Wonder's" example gave hope to dozens of American servicemen who returned home from the war as amputees.

Gray seemed to embody the underdog who could beat the odds on a regular basis because of his sheer confidence, guts and discipline. Not surprisingly, his aggressive play won the respect of the Philadelphia sportswriters, who honored him as the Most Courageous Athlete. With characteristic humility, Gray, when presented with the award, downplayed his personal struggle to become a professional baseball player and spoke instead of his tremendous respect for the American soldiers fighting abroad. "Boys, I can't fight," he admitted. "And so there is no courage about me. Courage belongs on the battlefield, not on the baseball diamond. But if I can prove to any boy who has been physically handicapped that he too can compete with the best—well, then, I've done my little bit."[21] The remark would become a trademark for Gray, who never really felt comfortable with his instant rise to fame or the issue of the soldier-amputee. He was basically a shy person who wanted to be left alone, but the press and the public would not allow it.

The War Department made movies of the one-armed outfielder at

One-Armed Wonder of the Southern Association, outfielder Pete Gray was an inspiration on and off the field. In 1944, he was voted MVP of the Southern Association for posting a .333 average, .996 fielding percentage and 68 stolen bases. Off the diamond, he visited army hospitals, encouraging servicemen who returned home from the battlefront as amputees. (Courtesy of Pete Gray.)

play in order to rejuvenate the spirits of amputees in veterans hospitals. Newsreels depicted his creative fielding technique for theater audiences across the nation, and feature articles appeared in *Time, The Saturday Evening Post,* and *The Sporting News.* Gray responded as best he could out of personal responsibility he felt to the American soldier and the general public.[22] He went on USO tours after completing the season, visiting army hospitals and rehabilitation centers. He spoke with recovering GIs, many of whom were amputees, reassuring them that they too could beat the odds and lead a healthy, happy, and productive life after the war.[23] In his attempt to fulfill all of those responsibilities, Pete Gray touched the heart of the nation.

Unlike the previous wars, the Korean conflict was limited in scope. Large-scale military conscription never took place. Instead, only a handful of individuals were drafted, usually one or two players per team, for a period of two years. This pattern continued throughout the decade of the 1950s, even after the Korean conflict ended in 1953. Because the Army go nearly all of the professional players who were drafted, it had some outstanding teams.[24] Stan Pawloski, who had just completed an All-Star season at Reading, was actually recruited by a captain at Fort Lee, Virginia, in 1952. "He called me up and said, 'Come down here, boy, and play ball for us,'" recalled the former Cleveland farm hand. "He was pretty insistent too. 'We're going to go down to Florida and train,' he told me. 'We'll play an 80-game schedule, and I'll tell you what, we get you here, it'll only be a two-year enlistment.' Sounded good to me, so I figured I'd take a chance. It's either that or get drafted and then you don't know where you're going or for how long."[25]

Palowski took the offer and entered special services. He spent the '53 season playing second base for Fort Lee, and improving his hitting. His ability to execute the hit-and-run was so remarkable that he was often compared to Hall of Fame second baseman Billy Herman of the Chicago Cubs. Together with Chet Nichols, who pitched for the Milwaukee Braves, and Harry Chiti, a catcher for the Chicago Cubs, Pawloski and his .432 batting average helped Fort Lee make it to the All-Army tournament in San Antonio, Texas, in 1953.[26] "Looking back on it, I'm not proud that I spent my time in the army in special services," he admitted. "Other guys who weren't baseball players didn't have that kind of advantage. But the experience allowed me to continue my career, and probably gave me more confidence as a hitter."[27]

Bob Duliba, who played service ball for the Marine Corps in the mid–1950s, also believes that the experience helped him once he returned stateside. "I had played minor league ball for three years before joining the Marines," he said. "But there were no pitching coaches back then, you were on your own. If you got any instruction, it came in spring training." Being shuttled back and forth between the high and low minors, Duliba became frustrated and left pro ball after the 1955 season. Enlisting in the Marine Corps, he was sent to Fort McPherson, Georgia, where he was immediately assigned to the ball club. "That's where I really learned to pitch," he admits. "In those days, we played 150 to 200 games a season because we had such great weather. I pitched every fourth or fifth day for three years, and faced some pretty good talent against Army teams, which were stacked with major leaguers. After a while you can't help but develop a touch mental approach to the game. If anything then, I was a 'hard thrower' in the minors. But the Marines made me a 'pitcher.'"[28]

Of the 21 men profiled in this book, 6 of them — Mathewson, Boley, Gazella, Ostrowski, Dorish and Chylak — served in a foreign conflict and three of them suffered injuries sustained during their service. They were true American heroes, on and off the ball diamond. Pawloski and Duliba enlisted and were assigned to special services, playing baseball and learning from the experience to help them in their quest to become major leaguers. And Paparella and Gray made a virtue out of a necessity. Both were deferred under the Selective Service Act and continued to pursue their baseball dreams, one as an umpire, the other as a symbol of hope for a nation at war.

It would be a mistake, however, to dismiss the other men in this book as having taken advantage of their status as professional ballplayers to avoid military service. Each and every one of them kept major league baseball alive for America and its soldiers during a time of national crisis. They served on the home front by boosting public morale, their heroics providing a symbolic solution to the daily frustrations of a war-weary nation.

5

Cooperstown Bound

Of the more than 100 northeastern Pennsylvanians who played, managed, or umpired in the major leagues, only six of them are enshrined in the National Baseball Hall of Fame in Cooperstown, New York. Five of those individuals were players—Hughie Jennings (whose major league career spanned the period 1891–1918); Christy Mathewson (1900–1916); Ed Walsh (1904–1917); Stan Coveleski (1912–1928) and Bucky Harris (1919–1931)—and only one, Nestor Chylak (1954–1979), was an umpire. Two of them, Mathewson and Walsh, were recently included among the top 100 greatest players of the 20th century by *The Sporting News,* and Matty enjoyed the singular honor of being named to Major League Baseball's All-Century team.[1]

The greatness of Jennings, Harris, Mathewson, Walsh, and Coveleski can easily be measured on the basis of five specific abilities. In baseball lingo, they are called the "tools" upon which every player is judged from the time he cracks the big leagues until the day he retires: the physical ability to run, throw, hit, hit for power, and field. But true greatness extends beyond even the most apparent physical gifts, being measured only after the first five tools have been decided. It is determined by intangible qualities, such as an understanding of how to get the most out of one's God-given talent; the perseverance to succeed in a game in which 70 percent failure is the mark of a very good hitter; and the discipline to conduct oneself with a respect for self, the game and its fans.

In granting baseball immortality, the National Baseball Hall of Fame recognizes both the physical abilities as well as the intangible qualities. To be eligible, a player must have played actively in the major leagues at some time during a period beginning 20 years prior to the annual election, and ending 5 years prior to the election. He must also have played in each of 10 championship seasons. Players are chosen for the Hall of Fame on the basis of "record, playing ability, integrity, sportsmanship, character, and contributions to the team(s) on which the player played." Any player receiving 75 percent of the vote in the annual election, either by the Baseball Writers Association or a special committee comprised of veteran players and baseball officials who have given long and meritorious service to the game, gains membership in the Hall of Fame.[2] True greatness then, is reserved for only the most outstanding individuals of the nearly 15,000 men who have donned a major league uniform.

Jennings, Harris, Mathewson, Walsh, and Coveleski not only possessed the necessary attributes to become Hall of Famers, but they played during an era that was conducive to their success. Their careers spanned the period 1891 to 1931, when the game was developing from largely rural, amateur pastime to a highly skilled professional game played in eastern cities. Pennsylvania's anthracite region became a proving ground for major league talent, allowing the anthracite leaguers to capture more easily the attention of big league scouts than it would be in a later generation when baseball expanded westward and the talent pool of prospects was just as talented, but much bigger. It was also a time of baseball "wars" in which the Western/American League and, later, Federal League, had come into existence challenging the superiority of the more established National League. The inter-league rivalry resulted in fluctuating player salaries, the raiding of rosters by other team owners in violation of the reserve clause, and, eventually the existence of a limited number of teams with a regular line-up.[3] In other words, the same pool of players were not only the objects of the inter-league rivalry, but also the ones establishing and breaking records almost on an annual basis.

Hughie Jennings's major league career is indicative of this rare combination of playing ability, intangible qualities, and historical circumstance. Having no minor league experience, Jennings went right from the anthracite leagues in 1890 to Louisville of the American Association in 1891. That season he hit a promising .292. The following year, however, he slumped to .222 against stronger pitching in the newly reorganized 12-team National League and was sold to the Baltimore Orioles. Under the tutelage of Ned Hanlon, part-owner and manager of the club, Jennings excelled, helping to establish one of baseball's earliest championship dynasties. The Orioles of the mid–1890s were one of the greatest collection of players ever assembled, featuring six future Hall of Famers: John J. McGraw, Wilbert Robinson, Joe Kelley, Dan Brouthers, Wee Willie Keeler and, of course, Jennings himself.

Starting in 1894, Baltimore captured three straight National League titles, winning its games through an exciting and rowdy style that featured intimidating the umpire, intentional spiking, insulting profanity, and such tricks as holding on to a base runner's belt to break his stride and hiding extra balls in the outfield grass. They were also a rugged, tough-minded bunch, playing despite injuries and illness.[4] Jennings and Baltimore were a perfect fit.

Refusing to back off the plate, Jennings led the league in being hit by pitched balls with 40 in his first year as an Oriole, only to improve the mark by 9 two years later. In 1897, he missed the last part of the season with a skull fracture, the result of yet another wild pitch. While the accident would have intimidated a lesser individual, the fiercely competitive Jennings returned to the line-up even stronger the next season, daring opposing hurlers to pitch him inside. In one game he was hit three straight times but the umpire refused to award him first base insisting that the scrappy infielder was being hit purposefully. During his fourth at-bat, Jennings was knocked clearly to the ground and given the bag. Taking to his feet, he cried out, "EE-yah," and danced down the line, grinning all the way.[5] He was just as exciting in the field.

In 1894, Baltimore and New York were battling it out for the National League championship. With two outs in the ninth inning of the deciding game and the Orioles leading by one run, the Giants loaded the bases. The batter hit a sharp line-drive over short, what appeared to be a certain base hit. While the runners began their sprint toward home plate, Jennings flung himself into the air, twisting and kicking, and somehow managed to snare the ball, giving Baltimore the championship.[6]

For the next three years, the Orioles were invincible and Jennings simply remarkable. He never hit below .328, achieving a high of .398 in 1896. Earning a reputation as the most dangerous clutch hitter in the game, Jennings also stole as many as 73 bases in a season and was the league leader in fielding average and put-outs three times each. According to Miller Huggins, who played and later managed against him, Jennings got as much as he could out of his limited abilities. "I always thought of him as a self-made player," admitted Huggins. "He didn't have as much natural ability as other men, but he taught himself and made himself a great player."[7]

Jennings also demonstrated that same exceptional drive in his personal life. Realizing that a career in major league baseball could easily be ended by a serious injury or string of bad luck, he returned to school

during his playing career. Not only did he attend St. Bonaventure College
in the off-season, but went on to study law at Cornell University, graduating in 1904. He was admitted to the bar in Maryland and Pennsylvania
and began practicing back home in Scranton in 1907.[8]

By 1897, Jennings's arm was weakening. He was eventually forced to
take three or four steps from his shortstop position in order to gain
momentum to throw to first on a routine play. No longer able to play deep,
he risked playing a shallow infield and relying on desperate dives to cut
off base hits. While he continued to hit .350 or better, his fielding percentage dropped to .929.[9] He was finished as a shortstop.

In 1899, when Hanlon left the Orioles to manage the Brooklyn
Dodgers, he took Jennings with him and converted the scrappy infielder
into a first baseman. The former anthracite leaguer led the Dodgers to
championships in 1899 and 1900, and captained the Philadelphia Phillies
in 1901 before embarking on a managerial career with the minor league
Baltimore Orioles.[10] Jennings is best remembered, however, as the colorful manager of the Detroit Tigers.

Between 1907 to 1920, he entertained fans from the first base coaching box by taunting the opposition with shouts, whistles and gyrations.
Rube Waddell, the eccentric pitching ace of the Philadelphia Athletics, was
a favorite target. "Jennings used to go to the dime store and buy little toys,
like rubber snakes or a jack-in-the-box," recalled Detroit outfielder Sam
Crawford. "He'd get in the first base coach's box and set them down on
the grass and yell, 'Hey, Rube, look!' Rube would look over at the jack-in-
the-box popping up and down and kind of grin, real slow-like, you know.
Yeah, Jennings would do anything to distract him from his pitching."[11]
Standing with both arms raised, fists doubled and one leg high in the air,
the Tiger's colorful manager would also encourage his own players with
a piercing yell of "At-a-boy," or "EE-yah," which became a trademark. Initially, Jennings used "EE-yah" to warn base runners of a pick-off attempt.
But when he discovered that the cry jarred opposing players, he adopted
it to antagonize as well, changing the tone to indicate triumph, warning,
jubilation, or anger. So popular was the cry that it was adopted by the
Allied European forces in World War I as they charged out of their bunkers
on the attack.[12]

Despite his animated, almost comical mannerisms, Jennings was no
buffoon. In fact, he was a strict disciplinarian with his players, the only
exception being the thin-skinned and volatile Ty Cobb, whom he gave
considerable latitude. Jennings saw in Cobb a good bit of the fire, grit and
desire he himself possessed as a player. Although they would feud over the
years, Jennings, early on, decided to let his young star do what he wanted
on the diamond.[13] To be sure, Cobb was Jennings's greatest asset as well as

liability in Detroit. Driven by seething ambition, the Georgia Peach angered most of the veterans on the team who tried to break his youthful arrogance by constantly chastising him and even attempting to force him off the club. "I let this go for a while because I wanted to satisfy myself that Cobb had as much guts as I thought in the very beginning," admitted Jennings. "Well, he proved it to me, and I told the other players to let him alone. He is going to be a great ballplayer some day and I won't allow him to be driven off this club. The next fellow who lays a hand on him will have to answer to me."[14]

Led by Cobb and an impressive pitching staff, Jennings and the Tigers captured three straight American League pennants. Unfortunately, they lost all three World Series, never again returning to the Fall Classic with the Scranton native at the helm. Jennings, who could be sarcastic and tempestuous, became increasingly unpopular with his players as his tenure — and second division finishes — unfolded. After completing the 1920 campaign in last place, he turned the managerial duties over to his protégé, Cobb, who downplayed his own insatiable desire for the job by praising his

As Detroit's manager, Hughie Jennings instructed his players and entertained fans from the coaching box with whistles, gyrations and shouts alike, "EE-yah!" and "At-a-boy!" (National Baseball Hall of Fame Library, Cooperstown, N.Y.)

former manager. "Jennings introduced a most attractive and wonderful spirit which seemed to inspire all the players under him," said Cobb, with an ironical twist. "He was liberal with me in all my career, never reprimanding me for a play and goodness knows I deserved plenty of them."[15]

Elected to the Hall of Fame in 1945, Jennings, by the end of his storied career, had compiled a career batting average of .312 and a very respectable 1,131-972 record as manager of the Detroit Tigers. The .398 batting average he posted in 1896 is still a major league record for shortstops.

Bucky Harris of the Washington Nationals was the youngest regular major league manager at age 27 and the team's second baseman. But like Jennings, who arranged for the scrappy youngster's first job in pro ball in 1915, Harris had an inauspicious beginning. When Harris first came up to Washington in 1919 as a 22-year-old second baseman, he was hardly impressive. He hit a lowly .214 and played in only eight games. Fortunately, he didn't have too much competition at second base in Ray Morgan, a .233 hitter, and Hal Janvrin, who barely hit his weight at .173. Owner Clark Griffith took a chance on Harris and made him the team's regular second baseman in 1920. It paid off. Not only did Harris hit .300, but he proved to be a fierce competitor who even had the audacity to stand up to the irascible Cobb.[16] In their very first encounter, the 6'1", 175-pound Cobb came flying into second base with his spikes high. Harris, all of 5'9" and 156 pounds, didn't flinch, slapping the Detroit star firmly on the chest with the tag.

"The next time you try that Busher," said Cobb, "I'll carve you like a turkey."

Undaunted by the threat, Harris, who was 10 years younger, replied: "The next time you come in at me like that, old man, I'm going to hit you right between the eyes with the ball."

Cobb, admittedly, respected the spunky infielder after that.[17]

Over the next three years, Harris would top American League second basemen in both put-outs and double plays and demonstrate an exceptional ability to steal bases. During the winter of 1923, when Harris was back home in Pittston playing professional basketball — in violation of his baseball contract — Griffith phoned to ask if he would be willing to shift to third base because a deal was in the works to bring Eddie Collins, the star second baseman of the Chicago White Sox, to Washington. Griffith also suggested that Collins would be his player-manager. A few weeks later, the crafty owner changed his mind and named Harris to the position. Critics called the move, "Griffith's folly," predicting that he would ruin a good, young infield by saddling the 27-year-old Harris with managerial duties. Nor was the job an especially attractive one.

Washington had been perennial tail-enders, inspiring the old saw, "First in war, first in peace and last in the American League." But with

Hughie Jennings was a strict disciplinarian with all of his players except the volatile and thin-skinned Ty Cobb, who eventually succeeded him as Detroit's manager in 1920. (Courtesy of the National Baseball Hall of Fame Library.)

Harris at the helm the Senators captured their first and only World Series in 1924, making the northeastern Pennsylvanian not only the youngest manager in the majors, but the youngest ever to capture a world championship.[18] The "Boy Manager," as he was called, led by example and timely hitting, earning the respect of seasoned players such as Walter Johnson, Sam Rice, Goose Goslin and Muddy Ruel. In the 1924 World Series against the New York Giants, Harris was at his very best. Not only did he set records for chances accepted, double plays and put-outs in the exciting seven-game affair, but he batted .333 and hit two home runs. Harris's two-run single in the eighth inning of Game Seven allowed Washington to tie the score at three runs apiece, sending the contest into extra innings. The Senators went on to win the game — and the Series— in the 12th.[19] It was also in that decisive game that the "Boy Manager" demonstrated his genius by replacing his right-handed starter, Curly Ogden, with left-hander George Mogridge in the first inning. The switch forced the Giants' hard-hitting

Bill Terry out of the line-up, eliminating one of their most dangerous hitters.[20]

One of Harris's most endearing qualities, however, was his love for the anthracite region. He returned during the off-season and as much as he could during the regular season. On September 12, 1924, for example, Harris, in the midst of a hotly contested pennant race, made time to bring the Senators to Exeter to play an exhibition game against the semi-pro Pittston Craftsmen. Arriving at 7:00 A.M. via the Lehigh Valley Railroad, the "Boy Manager" and his club were greeted by several hundred well-wishers. Nearly 6,000 fans packed the Exeter ballpark on Wyoming Avenue for the afternoon game, which Washington won, 15-5.[21]

Under Harris, the Senators repeated as American League champions in 1925, but lost a hard-fought, seven-game Series to the Pittsburgh Pirates. Although the Senators would post winning records for the next two seasons, the aging club slipped in the standings. After a fourth-place finish in 1928, Harris was traded to Detroit, where he was made a full-time manager. He spent five seasons (1929–33) with the Tigers, one with the Boston Red Sox, (1934), another eight (1935–42) with the Senators, and part of the 1943 season with the Philadelphia Phillies, never finishing higher than fourth place. His low-key approach won the players' loyalty while his exceptional knowledge for the game enabled him to get the most out of the available talent. Unfortunately, Harris rarely had the players he needed to contend. After managing in the minors for a few years, he returned to the majors as manager of the New York Yankees, leading the team to a World Series in 1947. He was named "Manager of the Year" by *The Sporting News*, only to be released after the following season when the Bronx Bombers finished a disappointing third. In 1950, Harris returned to Washington for a third tour of duty, finishing his managerial career, again, with Detroit in 1956.[22]

In his 29 seasons as manager, Bucky Harris collected 2 world championships, 3 pennants, 2,157 victories and 2, 218 defeats—a standard of futility exceeded only by Connie Mack's 3,948 losses as manager of the Philadelphia Athletics. Still the youngest man to lead a major league team to a World Series victory, Harris was elected, as a manager, to the Hall of Fame in 1975 by the Veterans Committee.[23]

The exceptional careers of Mathewson, Coveleski and Walsh can also be explained by historical circumstance as well as their own physical and intangible gifts. All three were pitchers who began their careers during the so-called Dead Ball Era, which lingered until 1920 when a livelier, cork-centered baseball was introduced and batting averages began to climb.[24] Before then, pitching decided games and hitting became almost a lost art. It was during that era that Christy Mathewson defined the standard of pitching excellence.

Stanley "Bucky" Harris of Pittston, who at the age of 27 led the Washington Senators to their only world championship, is the youngest man ever to lead a major league team to a World Series victory. (National Baseball Hall of Fame Library, Cooperstown, N.Y.)

No other pitcher was as talented, competitive or intelligent as Matty. Both John McGraw, the pugnacious manager of the New York Giants, and Connie Mack, the gentlemanly skipper of the Philadelphia Athletics, agreed that he was the greatest pitcher they had ever seen.[25] That said a lot, since both men were not only sparing with praise, but rarely agreed on anything. Matty possessed a good, though not overpowering, fast ball, an excellent curve and change of pace, and a "fade-away," or reverse curve ball, known to handcuff hitters in mid-swing. More important, he knew what pitch to throw and when, having an excellent memory for hitters' weaknesses.

The fortunes of the great New York Giants teams of the early 20th century rested largely on Mathewson's right arm. He won 20 games as a 21-year-old rookie in 1901. In his first appearance that season, Matty defeated the defending National League champion Brooklyn Dodgers on a four-hitter. He went on to win seven straight, including four shutouts before St. Louis defeated him on May 28. Behind the pitching of their raw-boned rookie, the Giants remained in the chase until July 4, before nose-diving into the second division. On July Mathewson no-hit the St. Louis Cardinals, before losing four straight. His arm was throbbing so painfully from overuse that he could hardly sleep at night. But he continued to pitch. On September 21, he defeated Cincinnati on a three-hitter for his 20th and final victory of the season.[26] It was a pattern that would haunt him throughout his career — some days he was simply unhittable and other days, usually after overuse, he would be hit hard.

After slumping to 14-17 the following season, Matty won 30 games in 1903 and led the National League with 267 strikeouts, a performance he would repeat for the next two seasons. His finest season came in 1908 when he led the league in wins (37), strikeouts (259), shutouts (12) and ERA (1.43). So effective was Mathewson that year that the sportswriters gave him the nickname, "Big Six," after the "Big Six Fire Company," the fastest one in New York City. Matty was at his best in the 1905 World Series when he shut out the Philadelphia Athletics in the first, third and fifth games, allowing a total of just 14 hits as the Giants captured the championship four games to one.[27] New York would return to the Series in 1911, 1912, and 1913, largely on the pitching exploits of Mathewson who won a total of 74 games during that three-year span. But Matty pitched into hard luck, winning only 2 of the 7 games he started in those three World Series. Nevertheless, those were great Giants teams, and Mathewson was the ace on each and every one.

"What a pitcher he was!" recalled John T. "Chief" Meyers, a full-blooded California Mission Indian who caught almost every game Mathewson pitched for seven years. "The greatest that ever lived. He had almost perfect control. Really almost perfect. You could sit in a rocking chair and

Christy Mathewson was the most dominant pitcher of his era, winning 30 or more games in four seasons and posting 20 or more victories in nine others. His 37 wins in 1908 still stand as a modern National League record. Nor has his three-shutout performance in the 1905 World Series against the Philadelphia Athletics ever been duplicated. (National Baseball Hall of Fame Library, Cooperstown, N.Y.)

catch Matty. In 1913 he pitched 68 consecutive innings without walking a man. That season he pitched over 300 innings and I doubt if he walked 25 men the whole year. Same thing in 1914. I don't think there was ever a time he couldn't throw that ball over the plate if he wanted to."[28] But Mathewson also had a sense of humor and was not averse to having fun on the mound, especially at his manager's expense. "There were times when Matty used to have McGraw sliding up and down the bench, getting madder by the second," recalled Meyers. "If he had a four- or five-run lead, he'd let up and lay the ball in there. He liked to see the outfielders run."[29]

In August 1911, when Mathewson suffered a five-game losing streak, the New York sportswriters began writing his obituary. There was one, however, who stood by the pitching legend. Ring Lardner, who elevated baseball writing to a literary art, defended Mathewson with a folksy, little essay:

> The boys been writin' subscriptions on his tombstone and namin' his pallbearers as far back as 1906, and they been layin' him to rest every year since. You've heard the old sayin' that a cat's got nine lives? Well, boys, Matty makes a cat look like a sucker.
>
> They called in a special doctor to look him over the last time the Giants went West. He couldn't sleep and they was a pain in his left arm, and his neck kept stiffenin' up on him. The special doctor says it was some kind o' nervous trouble. Great stuff. If Matty was goin' to be bothered with nervousness I guess it would have happened before this. Besides, do you think a stiff neck and a pain in the left arm and insomnia is goin' to stop him from pitchin'? His brain ain't diseased and he's still got the same right hand he always used.
>
> So give him a chanct. Don't talk like he was gone and ask me what kind of a pitcher *was* he. If you want to know what kind of a pitcher he *is*, I'll try to tell you.
>
> They's a flock o' pitchers that knows a batter's weakness and works accordin', but they ain't nobody else in the world that can stick a ball as near where they want to stick it as he can. I bet he can shave you if he wanted to and if he had a razor blade to throw instead of a ball.
>
> What makes him the pitcher he is? He's a tightwad with his stuff, and other pitchers is spendthrifts. Most of 'em want to whiff the big hitters and hear the crowd cheer. Matty'd rather have 'em hit the first ball and pop it up in the air.
>
> Then he's got this fade away that none o' the rest has got. But his fade away and his curve and his fast one and his control wouldn't be worth anything if he didn't know all he knows about pitchin'. He could write a whole sacklapedia on that subject and then not tell half he knows. So its the old bean that makes him what he is.[30]

Once again, the Giants' ace proved his critics wrong and completed the season with a 26-13 record and 141 strikeouts.

Mathewson also brought a much-needed touch of class to baseball in the game's formative years. Idolized by the fans and respected by both teammates and opponents, he became the first professional athlete to serve as a role model for youngsters.[31] Reserved by nature, Matty was, according to one teammate, "a little hard to get close to, but once you got to know him, he was a truly good friend."[32] His long-time catcher, Chief Meyers, insists that the Giants "loved to play for him." "We'd break our necks for that guy," he added. "If you made an error behind him, he'd never get mad or sulk. He'd come over and pat you on the back."[33]

At 6'1½" and 190 pounds, the blond-haired and blue-eyed Matty was uncommonly handsome and projected an image of sportsmanship and fair play in a sport that was considered rowdy and win-at-all-costs. Raised in a solid Protestant, middle-class family, he promised his mother that he wouldn't pitch on Sundays and rigidly adhered to that policy.[34] He was also a family man, who was devoted to his wife Jane and their only child, Christy Jr. Accordingly, Matty drank sparingly, considering it "an insult to assume that a good Christian gentleman could not refrain from excess drinking on his own," and had a reputation for being in bed before curfew.[35] "Never let it be said that there was a finer man than Christy Mathewson," remarked his boyhood friend, Ray Snyder, who Matty always remembered with a pair of tickets to every World Series game in which he pitched. "He never drank. He never smoked. He loved children, and was always proper."[36]

To be sure, Mathewson's clean-living reputation was exaggerated. He was known to argue with umpires, throw at hitters, and occasionally indulge in profanity. He smoked cigars and pipes, played poker regularly, and liked money, especially being the highest paid player in the game at $15,000 a year in 1911.[37] According to teammate Fred Snodgrass, Mathewson was "a terrific poker player," who "made a good part of his expenses every year at it." "I'm not saying he was a card shark, but that he could do *everything* well," added the Giants' center fielder.[38] But at a time when the press largely ignored the personal indiscretions of ballplayers and the public was hungry for a hero, Mathewson fit the image. A young Indiana farm boy by the name of Lloyd Lewis illustrates the point.

On October 24, 1911, Lewis decided to cut classes at a local Philadelphia college just to watch his "beloved Matty even the score with the Athletics," who were up two games to one in that year's World Series. Arriving early at Shibe Park, he took a seat near the railing along the right field line, which would that afternoon become the Giants' bullpen. When New York's ace pitcher took the field for his warm-up tosses, the adolescent found himself "pop-eyed, sitting not 20 feet away from the great Mathewson, who from the time I was 9 I had pretended I was, playing ball in the

Indiana cow pasture, throwing his famous 'fadeaway' which, for me, never came off." "I was let down for a minute," he admitted. "Matty didn't speak like a demigod, but as I stared, he looked it, all the same. He held up his head high, and his eye with slow, lordly contempt swept the Athletics as they warmed up across the field. He was 31, all bone and muscle and princely poise. Surely he would get those Athletics today and put the Giants back in the running." Unfortunately for Lewis, Mathewson and the Giants lost that day, 4-2, and the A's went on to clinch the Series by the same margin. After the game the collegian dragged himself forlornly to a nearby saloon.

"Two beers," he said, in his deepest voice.

"You ain't 21," the bartender rasped. But after another look, he saw how dejected the young man was. Taking pity on him, the barkeep splashed two great steins in front of him.

"Who's the extra one for?" he asked.

"Oh, that? That's for Mathewson," came the reply.[39]

When the Giants traded Mathewson, along with Edd Roush and Bill McKechnie, in 1916 to Cincinnati, it was, according to McGraw, to help his long-time friend and pitching ace fulfill a personal ambition to become a major league manager. "I don't like to part with Matty," insisted McGraw. "He was not only the greatest pitcher I ever saw — but he is my good friend. He could stay with the Giants as long as he wanted to but I'm convinced his pitching days are over and he'd like to be a manager. We've talked about it many times; I'd like to help him gratify that ambition."[40] Even so, it was a melancholy experience for Mathewson, who, while packing up his gear admitted, "I don't know whether I want to become the manager of another club or not. This locker is the only one I've ever had in my life." With tears in his eyes, Matty bid each of his teammates farewell and boarded a train for Cincinnati to become manager of the Reds.[41] After Mathewson's departure, Ring Lardner memorialized the event with six satirical but bittersweet lines:

> My eyes are very misty
> As I pen these lines to Christy
> Oh, my heart is full of heaviness today.
> May the flowers ne'er wither, Matty
> On your grave at Cincinnati
> Which you've chosen for your final fadeaway.[42]

Mathewson was a first-ballot Hall of Fame selection in the charter class of 1936, mesmerizing the baseball writers with his statistical totals. He was clearly the most dominant pitcher of his era, winning 30 or more games in four seasons and posting 20 or more victories in nine others. His 37 wins in 1908 still stand as a modern National League record and his three straight, 30-win streak from 1903 to 1905 has been matched only once. But his three-shutout 1905 World Series performance against Connie Mack's Philadelphia Athletics has never been duplicated. At the end of his stellar career, Matty had compiled 372 victories (fourth all-time), 78 shutouts (third), and a 2.13 ERA (fifth).[43]

Ed Walsh might have challenged the remarkable career totals posted by Mathewson if he had a little less swagger and considerably more restraint. Nicknamed "Big Ed" because of his 6'1", 193-pound size and powerful delivery, Walsh was one of the most prolific workhorse pitchers of the early 20th century. But he was also a cocky, fun-loving charmer, who never refused an opportunity to take the mound. An above-average fast ball got him to the majors with the Chicago White Sox in 1904.[44] But it was a devastating spitball that made him a Hall of Famer.

Like a split-fingered fast ball, Walsh's spitter dropped sharply before crossing the plate, making it almost impossible to hit. According to Sam Crawford of Detroit, Big Ed's spitball "disintegrated on the way to the

"Big Ed" Walsh of Plains, considered a "workhorse pitcher," hurled a total of 2,526 innings between 1906 and 1912. In 1908 alone, Walsh posted a 40-15 record, winning 45.5 percent of the Chicago White Sox's 88 victories—the highest percentage of an American League team's wins in history. (National Baseball Hall of Fame Library, Cooperstown, N.Y.)

plate and the catcher put it back together again." So effective was the pitch that the Tiger's hitting great swore that when it crossed the plate "it was just the spit that went by."[45] Walsh toyed with the pitch, perfecting not one, but four different ways to throw it. "Depending on my grip, I could break the pitch four different ways," he once admitted. "Let's take a right-handed hitter. I could break the ball down and away, straight down, down and in, and up. To get the rise, I threw underhand, but the three other pitches were thrown with the same motion as my fast one. I'd grip the ball with the fingers close together and the thumb underneath. I let the ball slip from under my wet fingertips. Learning the release is the trick to mastering the spitter."[46] Nor did Walsh rely solely on the spitter, alternating the pitch with his fast ball.

"When I loaded up the spitter I kept the glove in front of my mouth so I could bluff the pitch," he explained. "I didn't throw it on every pitch. I averaged two or three to every hitter. The other times I relied on the fast ball, which I threw with the same motion. In fact, I believe that my spitter was as effective as it was because it looked like a fast ball until it got within four or five feet of the plate. Then it would break sharply, fooling the hitter in mid-swing."[47]

Between 1906 and 1912, Walsh pitched 2,526 innings. During five of those seasons he threw at least 32 complete games and his single season ERA was never above 2.22. Posting a 17-13 record and an 1.88 ERA in 1906, Walsh led the "Hitless Wonder" White Sox to the World Series, where he blanked the Chicago Cubs on two hits in Game Three and proved victorious again in Game Five. He also struck out at least 250 hitters each season between 1908 and 1912, throwing a no-hitter against the Boston Red Sox in 1911.[48]

Walsh's finest season, however, came in 1908 when he posted a 40-15 record, winning 45.5 percent of Chicago's 88 games. It was the highest percentage of an American League team's wins in history. He also led the league in games (66), innings pitched (465), complete games (42), winning percentage (.727), shutouts (12), and strikeouts (269).[49] It was also during that same season that Walsh enjoyed what he called his "greatest day in baseball"—October 8, 1908. "On that day," he recalled, "I fanned Larry Lajoie of the Cleveland Indians with the bases full and the White Sox chances for the pennant hanging on every pitch. With two outs and bases loaded in the ninth, Larry comes to the plate. I got strike one off a spitball that he hit foul down the third base line. My next pitch was a spitter on the outside part of the plate. Larry swung and tipped it foul back to the stands. Strike two. Then I threw him an overhand fast ball that raised and he watched it come over without even an offer. Strike three. Lajoie sort of grinned at me and tossed his bat toward the bench without even a word. We won that game

3-2, in the last days of a three-way pennant race and though we didn't take the pennant that year, I still consider that strike-out the high spot of my career."[50]

Walsh never again reached the dizzying heights of that 1908 season, though he did post consecutive 27-win records and tallied a 168-112 record over the next seven years. Through it all, he battled a tired arm. In 1912, after throwing 42 innings in 10 days to clinch the World Series, Big Ed allegedly said that he wanted to rest his arm for a full year. When asked why he returned to the mound during spring training the following year, he replied: "The White Sox needed me — implored me to return — so I did."[51] It was a mistake.

He was hit like never before in 1913. Limited to 16 games that season, Walsh pitched just 98 innings. "I could feel the muscles grind and wrench during the game, and it seemed to me that my arm would leap out of the socket when I shot the ball across the plate," he said years later. "My arm would keep me awake til morning with a pain that I had never known

Stan Coveleski pitched in the major leagues for 14 years, compiling an impressive 215-142 record, 39 shutouts, a 2.88 ERA, and six straight seasons pitching 276 innings or more. (National Baseball Hall of Fame Library, Cooperstown, N.Y.)

before."[52] During the next three years, he would pitch in just 13 games, ending his career with the Boston Braves in 1917.

Elected to the Hall of Fame by the Veterans Committee in 1946, Walsh's 195-126 career record was impressive, but the 1.82 ERA he posted over 14 seasons was the best in modern history. [53]

Stan Coveleski was also a spitballer and was one of the few hurlers permitted by major league baseball to throw the pitch after it was outlawed in 1920.[54] He broke into the majors with Connie Mack's A's in 1912. "Went up to Philadelphia in September and played in three games that year," recalled the Shamokin native. "Ben Ames caught me that first game. Told me, 'All you have to do is throw it right at my glove and I'll give you a mark.' So I pitched and gave them just three hits. Shut 'em out, 3-0! But the A's already had [Eddie] Plank, [Chief] Bender and [Jack] Coombs. Don't know if I could have beat them out for a spot in the rotation. Mack didn't think so and let me go. I know he was sorry afterwards."[55]

In 1916, Coveleski began a nine-year career with Cleveland, where he posted 4 straight 20-win seasons and a total record of 172-123. A control pitcher who averaged one walk every 3.86 innings over 14 years, Coveleski, in one game, pitched 7⅔ 3 innings without throwing a single ball. Every pitch that wasn't hit went over the plate for a strike. His most memorable performance though came in the 1920 World Series against the Brooklyn Dodgers. He pitched three complete games, allowing just two runs in 27 innings and winning all three games. His incredible ERA of .67 still stands as a World Series record.[56] A quiet, unassuming man, Coveleski's humility belied his remarkable success. "Won three complete games in the 1920 Series," he once said. Quickly dismissing the achievement, he confessed that "those games were just like any others to me. When I walked back to the clubhouse afterwards, nobody really said anything to me. I guess it was expected."[57] Despite his success with Cleveland, Covey really didn't like playing there. When asked about his feelings years later, he refused to elaborate, saying: "The best thing that happened to me there was pitching to Steve O'Neill. He caught me for nine years in Cleveland and knew me so well that he didn't even need to give me a sign."[58]

In 1925 Coveleski was traded to Washington where he played for another anthracite league product, Bucky Harris. That season he posted a 20-5 record, including a 13-game winning streak, and finished the campaign with a league-leading 2.84 ERA. He also made a second, less successful World Series appearance, losing two games to the Pittsburgh Pirates.[59] "That 1925 team was a good hitting team, but nobody could field," recalled the spitballer. "So Bucky counted on the pitching and his own strategy to get us through. He'd come up to me between innings when I was pitching and go over the next inning's hitters. And, by God, if I threw those hitters just like he told me, our fielders— as bad as they were — would have two or three steps on that ball before it was hit! Bucky sure was a smart manager and a good man to play for, too."[60]

Loyal to family and friends, Covey refused to pitch against his older brother, Harry, who pitched for the Detroit Tigers. In fact, Harry

When he pitched for Cleveland, Stan Coveleski (right), fiercely loyal to his family, refused to pitch against his older brother Harry Coveleskie (left), who was with Detroit, for fear of defeating him and causing ill feelings. (National Baseball Hall of Fame Library, Cooperstown, N.Y.)

Coveleski was quite a pitcher in his own right. As a young pitcher for the Phillies, he earned the moniker "Giant Killer" in 1908 when he defeated John McGraw's Giants three times in the span of five days, eliminating New York's chances to win the National League pennant. "They say McGraw never forgave him for that," said Stan, proudly. "They also say that the Giants ran him out of the league the following season. What a lot of bull that is. Nobody ever ran Harry out of any league. What happened was that he got hurt the next season. Went back down to the minors for a few years. But his arm came back and he pitched for Detroit while I was with Cleveland. They always wanted us to pitch against each other, but we refused. Wouldn't do it, and they never forced it."[61]

Covey pitched for Washington in 1926 and for part of the 1927 campaign before signing with the Yankees. His effectiveness declined, the result of a chronically sore arm. In 1928, he helped the Bronx Bombers to another pennant with a 5-1 record in 12 appearances. It was his final season in the majors. Elected to the Hall of Fame in 1969 by the Veterans Committee, his career totals included an impressive 215-142 record, 39 shutouts, six straight seasons pitching 276 innings or more, and a 2.88 ERA.[62]

If Jennings, Harris, Mathewson, Walsh and Coveleski had anything in common, it was their remarkable durability and incredible work ethic, traits that were cultivated during their childhoods in the anthracite region. Nestor Chylak, who was elected to the Hall by the Veterans Committee in 1999, possessed the same qualities. He umpired in the major leagues for more than 25 years and was selected to officiate in five World Series, six All-Star games and three American League Championship Series.[63] Chylak worked at umpiring year-round, quoting rules numerically by section and paragraph and staying in shape by playing handball. He also used dancing in order to develop his timing. "When you're getting into position to make a call, if you don't have timing, you're going to make a mistake," he explained.[64]

While Chylak had an air of confidence that let managers and players know he was in charge of the game, he avoided lengthy arguments. He understood that fans paid to see the players, not to watch the spectacle of an argument with the umpire. According to Hall of Fame third baseman Brooks Robinson of the Baltimore Orioles: "Nestor was my favorite umpire because he let you have your say and go about your business. He was also the best at calling balls and strikes. I always felt that the best umps are the ones you never heard about, but simply went about their jobs. That was Nestor. He was terrific."[65] Yogi Berra agreed. "Nestor was very good to work with because he was always in control of the game," said the Yankee legend. "Sometimes he would ask me, 'Did I miss this one or that one, Yog?' I'd say, 'No, you were right.' Then, when he did miss one and I told him about it, he was very reasonable. He'd say, "I got to do better next time.'"[66] Above all, Chylak managed to keep his composure at times when the players and fans were out of control.

On June 14, 1974, for example, unruly fans stormed the field at Cleveland's Municipal Stadium during the ninth inning of "Beer Night," when the beverage was discounted to 5¢ a cup. The game was tied, 5-5, at the time. In the melee that occurred, someone ripped out a chair from the stands and hurled it onto the field. Chylak suffered a cut wrist, but managed to restore peace temporarily. When another fan fight broke out near the pitcher's mound, Nestor ended the game, declaring Texas the winner by forfeit.[67]

Nestor Chylak umpired in the American League for 25 years. Selected to officiate in five World Series, six All-Star Games, and three League Championship Series, the Olyphant native possessed an air of confidence that let managers and players know he was in charge of the game. (National Baseball Hall of Fame Library, Cooperstown, N.Y.)

Like the other anthracite Hall of Famers, Chylak always remembered family and friends. Whenever he umpired a game in New York he made sure to drive home to Dunmore to be with his family, if only for a few hours. One of the most memorable occasions came on May 10, 1958, when he was officiating at Yankee Stadium and looked up at the scoreboard to discover that his wife had just given birth to their first son. When his children became older, he often took them to spring training or on east-coast road trips during the summer so he could spend time with them.[68] Among friends he was considered one of baseball's greatest ambassadors. A popular speaker in the off-season, Chylak extolled the virtues of the national pastime before community groups and gave away baseballs, bats and other memorabilia to kids.[69] One of those youngsters was an 11-year-old boy from Scranton with cirrhosis of the liver. Chylak, who bartended in the off-season, held a fund raiser to pay for a liver transplant at a local tavern. Afterwards, he signed a baseball for the child that read: "Be fair and play hard, Best Wishes, Nestor Chylak."[70]

All six of these northeastern Pennsylvanians set a standard of play-ing excellence, integrity, and service to the game of baseball. But it's inter-esting to note that with the exceptions of Mathewson and Jennings, all the others were elected to the Hall of Fame by the Veterans Committee. If their elections had been dependent on the Baseball Writers Association of Amer-ica — which is known to have an incredibly short-term memory, often ignoring those who played prior to 1920 — it is doubtful that the other four would have been inducted at all.[71] More tragic is the fact that Jake Daubert, Buck Freeman, and Steve O'Neill possess better career totals than many of their contemporaries who have been granted baseball immortality. But as their careers recede further into the distant past, it is doubtful that even the Veterans Committee will grant them a bronze plaque.

The "politics of glory" are, indeed, fickle when it comes to the base-ball-playing sons of the anthracite region. If there is any justice in the cur-rent voting system, perhaps Daubert, Freeman and O'Neill will one day receive their due. If not, then perhaps northeastern Pennsylvania will estab-lish its own Hall of Fame and acknowledge their contributions to the national pastime.

6

Living the Dream

There is a supreme irony in the professional careers of the ballplayers who came from Pennsylvania's anthracite region. By cracking the majors they had entered an industry that was, in principle, strikingly similar to the one they sought to escape back home in the coal pits of northeastern Pennsylvania. Baseball's early history, in particular, was dominated by an economic structure and labor relations that mirrored those of the anthracite industry. In both cases, owners were entrepreneurs seeking upward mobility at the expense of the workers, who were deprived control over their wages, working conditions, and terms of employment.[1] While the coal miners responded by forming a union and using the strike as a negotiating tool, ballplayers were essentially reduced to a species of peonage because Congress and the courts declined to force baseball to conform to such labor practices as collective bargaining. In baseball, contracts were negotiated individually and there existed radically unequal bargaining power between clubs and players due to the reserve clause. Nor did a strong players' union exist until the 1960s.[2]

Initially, the players pitted owners against each other by jumping to renegade leagues that offered greater salaries, or enhanced their wages by cavorting with gamblers intent on fixing the World Series. But with the creation of the National Agreement in 1903, and the installation of a commissioner with autocratic supervisory powers in the wake of the 1919 Black

91

Sox Scandal, the players were forced to abide by the game's internal legal and economic structure.[3]

Most of the players who came from the anthracite region — like the vast majority of major leaguers— showed very little dissatisfaction with the system, being grateful simply for the opportunity to escape the coal mines and earn a living by playing a game they truly loved. Buck Freeman, for example, was more concerned with establishing himself as a bona fide star than with the salary he was paid.

A left-handed pitcher converted to the outfield because of his remarkable hitting, Freeman was one of the premier sluggers of the Dead Ball Era and the proto-type for Babe Ruth. In 1899 — his first full season in the majors— the Wilkes-Barre native hit 25 home runs to lead the National League, a record that would stand until 1919 when Ruth collected 29 round-trippers.[4] "The hometown fans love to watch opposing outfielders when Freeman comes to bat," reported the *Washington Evening Star.* "Those fielders, who stand immobile most of the time, turn and run about 20 feet towards the fences."[5]

After moving to the Boston Red Sox in the newly formed American League in 1901, Freeman was among the regular leaders in home runs and RBI for the next three years. His clutch hitting also carried the Red Sox to two pennants (1903 and 1904) and victory in the first modern World Series in 1903. When compared to his Hall of Fame contemporaries, those achievements are just as deserving of a bronze plaque at Cooperstown. But Freeman has never been given serious consideration for the honor. Nor was he paid market value during his career.

Despite his impressive contributions, Freeman never made more than $1,500 a season at a time when star players on other clubs were earning $2,000 or more.[6] Considering, on the other hand, that annual wages for coal miners at the turn of the century ranged from $210 to $616, with a mean of about $375, Freeman fared much better than those who toiled in the anthracite pits.[7]

Eddie Murphy, an honest member of the 1919 Black Sox, was exploited even more than Freeman, having to play for Charles Comiskey, who is still considered to have been the most greedy of all baseball moguls. Murphy began his major league career as a part-time player in 1912 with the Philadelphia Athletics. In 33 games he hit an impressive .317 for a club that was building a championship dynasty. The following season Murphy was made a regular in the outfield, and the A's returned to the World Series against John McGraw's New York Giants. Murphy collected five hits in the Fall Classic, one coming off Christy Mathewson, as the A's defeated the Giants four games to one. His star continued to rise in 1914 when he stole 36 bases and was among the American League's leaders in walks and runs scored.

Murphy also collected three hits, including two doubles, in the World Series that year.[8] But the A's lost to the "Miracle" Boston Braves four games to one, in what some believe to have been a "fix."[9] Amid rumors that many of his players were cavorting with the renegade Federal League, Mack, rather than pay his stars their new market value, broke up the dynasty.[10]

Murphy was one of the last to go, not departing until July 16, 1915. "We were in Chicago that day," he remembered, "and Mr. Mack came to me on the field before the game and said, 'I'd like you to meet Clarence Rowland, manager of the White Sox.' We went under the stands, and when I shook hands with Rowland, he said, 'You ought to know we just bought you.' So I went into the club house and changed uniforms."[11]

Comiskey reportedly paid just $13,500 for the young outfielder, while shelling out $50,000 for the A's great second baseman Eddie Collins, who had been sold to Chicago earlier in the year.[12] The White Sox owner was known to spend considerable money on acquiring top talent, but his lavishness ended when it came to paying his players. "Shoeless Joe" Jackson, for example, was considered the greatest natural hitter in the game and regularly hit .350 or higher. But for all his ability, Comiskey refused to pay his star outfielder more than $6,000 a year, about half of what lesser stars on other clubs were earning. Similarly, third baseman Buck Weaver — a career .333 hitter — never earned more than $6,000 a year.[13] Accordingly, Murphy, who was a reserve player, probably earned considerably less.

Worse, Comiskey, like the coal magnates of northeastern Pennsylvania, invented creative ways to cut his costs at the expense of the players. While other teams gave their players four dollars a day for meals, the White Sox owner only paid three. He also charged players 50¢ for cleaning their uniforms — a courtesy in all other major league clubhouses. Those players who rebelled by wearing soiled uniforms had them taken from their lockers and cleaned for an additional charge.[14] But Comiskey's greed didn't seem to affect Murphy, who continued to show great promise as a hitter after being sold to Chicago.

In 70 games for the 1915 Sox, the former anthracite leaguer batted .315. Used primarily as an outfield reserve and pinch hitter for the next five years, Murphy hit a career high .486 in 30 games for the 1919 White Sox, widely considered to be one of the greatest teams ever. Infamously dubbed the "Black Sox," Chicago, in retaliation for Comiskey's greediness, threw the World Series that year, losing five games to three to the Cincinnati Reds. The following year Judge Kenesaw Mountain Landis, the newly appointed commissioner of baseball, banned from the game for life eight members of the team for conspiring with gamblers, including pitcher Eddie Cicotte, third baseman Buck Weaver, and outfielder "Shoeless Joe" Jackson — all potential Hall of Famers.[15]

1919 Chicago Black Sox. "Honest Eddie" Murphy (pictured in back row, third from right) was an outfield reserve and pinch hitter for the team, widely considered to be one of the greatest teams ever before throwing the 1919 World Series to the Cincinnati Reds. Among those banned from the game for life for their involvement in the fix were Eddie Cicotte (seated on the ground, first on right); Buck Weaver (seated in middle row, first on right); and "Shoeless Joe" Jackson (standing in back row, first on left). (Courtesy of Eddie Murphy, Jr.)

Murphy did not participate in the fix, earning himself the name "Honest Eddie."[16] But he did share in the cover-up, along with other innocent players like Eddie Collins, Ray Schalk and Dickie Kerr. When asked about the scandal years later he admitted: "There were cliques on the club, and the eight who were thrown out always hung around together, even at the batting cage. During batting practice our gang stood in one group, waiting for our turn to hit, and their gang had their own group. We knew something was wrong for a long time, but we felt we had to keep silent because we were fighting for a pennant. We went along and gritted our teeth and played ball. It was tough."[17]

Murphy's reluctance to reveal the scandal was most likely due to his friendship with Jackson. He sympathized with the South Carolinian because of his limited education and believed that Jackson was "easily led" by the ringleaders.[18]

While Freeman and Murphy may not have challenged the status quo, Jake Daubert did, repeatedly, insuring that he would be treated fairly and paid market value. A two-time National League batting champion with the

Brooklyn Dodgers, he was a steady .300 hitter for 10 years of the Dead Ball Era. He was also considered the league's best all-around first baseman, never fielding below the .989 mark and averaging 10.5 chances per game during that same time period. Those exceptional statistics make Daubert the most outstanding first baseman *not* in the Hall of Fame.[19] The omission is due, in part, to the active — and controversial — role he played in baseball's early labor relations, which earned him a reputation as a "troublemaker" among the owners.

Knowing his value to the Dodgers, Daubert refused to be exploited and pioneered baseball's fledgling unionization movement. In 1913 he became the vice-president and director of the Baseball Players' Fraternity, which lobbied the three-man National Baseball Commission for better labor conditions. In November, Daubert and the fraternity's president, David Fultz, drafted and presented to the Commission a petition with the following requests[2]:

1. Permission for a player to negotiate with any club after he is given his unconditional release.
2. That a club provide 10 days notice before a player is unconditionally released.
3. To inform a player of the terms of his new contract when sent to another team.
4. That a veteran player not be sent to a minor league team when his services interest another major league club.
5. That clubs furnish free to players their uniforms and shoes.
6. That travel expenses be paid between the players' homes and spring training camps.
7. To inform a player in writing of any fine or suspension levied against him.

Daubert believed that the requests were "reasonable and framed after a great deal of careful consideration of all angles — not just the players'." But he was also a realist and understood that "organized ball will simply delay its decision indefinitely and eventually shelve them altogether," which is, in fact, what happened.[21] Undeterred by the rebuff, he continued to battle the Commission — and ownership — for better conditions as well as pay.

When competition with the Federal League resulted in an increased salary scale, Daubert sought and received a $4,000 increase from Dodger owner Charles Ebbetts. But when the Commission shortened the 1918 season to accommodate the World War I crisis and tried to prorate salaries, Daubert sued Ebbetts for the unpaid balance of $2,150 and received most of it in a settlement. Furious over the incident, Ebbetts traded the Shamokin native to Cincinnati in 1919, where he helped lead the Reds to a pennant and a tarnished world championship against the Black Sox.[22]

Throughout his major league career, Daubert saved his money and was able to invest in a coal washery along the Schuylkill River, which secured his financial future.[23] But that didn't stop him from holding out in 1922 when Cincinnati owner August Herrmann offered him a two-year contract at less than the single-season figure of $10,500, which he had earned the year before. Herrmann insisted that he was "taking a risk" on the 38-year-old Daubert because of his age.[24] A compromise was reached and the former coal miner returned to the Reds for another three seasons, two of which proved to be among his most productive in the majors. In 1922, he collected 205 hits for a .336 average, scored 114 runs, and hit 12 homers, while leading the league in triples (22), put-outs (1,652) and fielding average (.994). The following season his batting average dropped to .292, but he was still among the league's leaders in put-outs (1,224) and fielding average (.993).[25]

During the 1920s and 1930s, players became more willing to challenge the sport's one-sided economic structure which favored the owners. The Roaring Twenties, in particular, was a decade of booming prosperity. An expanding urban population, declining work hours, and hefty increases in recreational spending by the American public created a sparkling turnabout in the

A two-time National League batting champion with the Brooklyn Dodgers, Jake Daubert was a steady .300-hitter for 10 years of the Dead Ball Era. With a career fielding percentage of .989, he was also one of the bets first basemen in the league. But his active role in pioneering baseball's first unionization movement has prevented him from gaining election to the Hall of Fame (National Baseball Hall of Fame Library, Cooperstown, N.Y.)

game's fortunes, making it the national pastime.[26] With the autocratic power of the commissioner firmly established, however, players worked within the legal constraints of the system to better their financial circumstances. At a time when the reserve clause tied a player to one club until ownership decided to trade, sell or release him, their efforts were often fruitless, the big money being limited to only a few. Chief among them was Babe Ruth of the New York Yankees.

Ruth was both a product as well as a catalyst of the Roaring Twenties. Not only did he revolutionize the game with his power hitting, being the first player to hit 30, 40, 50 and 60 home runs in a season, but was the prototype of the modern superstar. Because of his hitting exploits the Yankees were perennial contenders, if not World Series champions, during the decade of the twenties. Outgoing and boisterous, Ruth loved being the center of attention. His image appeared on everything from advertisements for men's underwear to baseball cards. He starred in silent films and rodeos, and he quickly won over the affections of youngsters, beginning a cult of hero worship among sports figures that still continues today.[27] Predictably, northeastern Pennsylvanians were Yankee fans, and Ruth, the hero of popular choice. Even those anthracite products who made it to the majors were judged on their relationship to Ruth and the Yankees. What that meant was their ability to secure a spot on New York's roster, or alternatively, defeat the Yankees and their marquee player as an opponent. Mike Gazella of Olyphant, for example, played only four years in the major leagues. He was a utility infielder with a career batting average of .241. Though he never saw more than 66 games worth of playing time in a season, his entire career was spent with the Yankees, and for that he was considered a hometown hero in the coal region.

Signed by the great Yankee scout Paul Krichell in 1923, "Gazook," as he was called, knew the value of a dollar and manipulated the payscale to his advantage. When the Yankees gave him just $500 for signing, he entertained a $5,000 offer from Connie Mack of the A's who tried to lure him away. Gazella turned down Philadelphia's legendary manager, but not before informing Yankee owner Jacob Ruppert of the offer and extricating an additional $1,000 from him.[28]

Gazella played in just eight games that year, before being sent down to the minors. When he returned to the Yanks in 1926, he became an important back-up to the aging "Jumpin' Joe" Dugan at third base. That year the Yankees went to the Series against the St. Louis Cardinals. In Game Five — the only one in which he played — Gazella was hit by a pitch in the 10th inning to load the bases and later made the final out in a fine defensive play, to seal the 3-2 victory for the Bronx Bombers.[29] When the team voted him just a quarter share of the Series money because he

Although he never saw more than 66 games' worth of playing time, Mike Gazella's entire four-year major league career was spent with the New York Yankees, a fact that allowed him to bask in the reflected glory of "Murderer's Row" long after his career had ended. (National Baseball Hall of Fame Library, Cooperstown, N.Y.)

appeared in only 66 games, Gazella held out for a full share. Backed by Manager Miller Huggins, he took his case to Commissioner Landis who ordered the players to pay him his full share, which they did.[30]

Gazella supplemented his income at the card table, where he had something of a reputation as a "shark." Once Babe Ruth asked him to play a hand of poker, but after the Bambino lost $67, he knew better than ever to ask again.[31] By the end of his four-year career, which included four trips to the World Series, Gazella earned over $50,000 in series money, which wasn't bad for a utility infielder who played in just 160 games during his entire big league career.[32]

Joe Shaute of Peckville, on the other hand, became a folk hero in the anthracite region because of his exceptional pitching against the Yankee slugger Babe Ruth. Shaute spent 13 years in the majors, mostly with the Cleveland Indians. When he made his debut in September 1922, Ruth was the first hitter he faced. The game was being played at New York's Polo Grounds and the Indians were clinging to a one-run lead in the bottom of the eighth with two outs and bases loaded with Yankees. "Don't get nervous just because the big fellow is up, Joe," said Tris Speaker, Cleveland's manager, as he handed him the ball. "Just pitch him like you would any other home run hitter ... carefully!"

Shaute struck out the Great Bambino on four pitches to end the inning. The following inning he faced Bob Meusel, another dangerous power hitter. The Yankee outfielder swung so hard on Shaute's first offering that he whirled completely around and fell to the ground. "This big league pitching is pretty soft," Shaute thought to himself. "It's no tougher then when I was throwing them by hitters in the minors. Meusel looked so bad on that pitch, I'll give him another one in the same location." He did — and Meusel parked it in the left field bleachers. So did New York's catcher Freddie Hoffman a few minutes later.[33] But the Peckville native continued to dominate Ruth for the next three years.

"I really had a whammy on the Babe," he admitted. "I was pretty cocky when we faced each other because I knew I could overpower him. I guess all that confidence paid off."[34] Shaute's luck changed in 1927, though. That season Ruth smacked 60 home runs to set a major league record that would stand for more than 70 years. Three of those round-trippers came off Shaute, numbers 30, 40 and 52. Still, over the course of his 13 seasons in the big leagues, the Peckville southpaw struck out Ruth more than 30 times.[35]

Shaute's best season came in 1924 when he won 20 games for the lowly Indians who finished sixth that year. At the end of the season, Cleveland owner James Dunn gave his pitcher a $1,000 bonus. But Shaute insisted that his performance was worth more. Before spring training, he managed

Joe Shaute of Peckville spent 13 years in the majors, mostly with Cleveland. He is best remembered for his success against Babe Ruth, whom he struck out more than 30 times. (National Baseball Hall of Fame Library, Cooperstown, N.Y.)

to wrangle another $2,000 out of Dunn, in addition to his base salary of $6,000. "When you consider how short a major league career is and the risks a player takes, a man should bargain for what he thinks he's worth," insisted the Cleveland pitcher. "At the same time, he should be prepared to deliver for the sum he's paid," he added.[36] Unfortunately for the Indians, Shaute won only 4 games while dropping 12 the following season. Nor would he ever win more than 14 for the Tribe again. Traded to Brooklyn in 1931, he was used primarily as a reliever, finishing his career with Cincinnati in 1934.[37]

Shaute credits whatever success he had as a pitcher to his catcher Steve O'Neill, another anthracite product. "The summer I won those 20 games for the Indians, Steve caught virtually every game," he recalled years later. "He also taught me how to decoy my pitches, which allowed me to become an effective pitcher. He really did a lot for me, more than I can ever acknowledge."[38] O'Neill himself belongs in the Hall of Fame, having forged a remarkable 17-year career in the majors.

A star catcher for Cleveland, O'Neill caught more than 100 games nine consecutive seasons (1915–23) and batted .311 or better each year from 1920 through 1922. His expert handling of a remarkable pitching staff earned him the praise of the team's ace, Hall of Famer Stan Coveleski. Not surprisingly, O'Neill was behind the plate for all seven games of the Indians' 1920 World Series victory, while also hitting .333 in the Fall Classic.[39] Considering the physical abuse a catcher takes behind the plate, those statistics are exceptional, placing him on par with Ray Schalk of the Chicago White Sox and Rick Ferrell of the Washington Senators, both of whom are in the Hall of Fame.[40]

Just as exceptional was O'Neill's fierce loyalty to family and friends and the work ethic he learned as a youngster. Those qualities were forged in the coal pits of northeastern Pennsylvania, where he returned to work in the off-season in order to support his family.[41] When he hit a two-run double in the 1920 World Series to give Cleveland a 3-1 victory in Game One, O'Neill's thoughts were with his friends back home. "As I stood on second base, I was thinking of the big scoreboard in front of the old *Scranton Times* building and the hundreds of people jamming Spruce Street," he said. "My friends were out in that crowd. They were the fellows with whom I worked in the coal breaker and in the coal mines and the fellows with whom I went to grade school. They watched the scoreboard operator put my name beside the 'At Bat' sign, and now the operator was moving that little figure from home plate to second base, showing that I had doubled. I could hear the roar and, at last, a boyhood dream had come true."[42] Hughie Jennings, who gave O'Neill his first break in professional baseball, once hailed the Minooka native as "the greatest catcher of the era"

Steve O'Neill of Minooka caught more than 100 games each season for nine straight years (1915–23) and batted .311 or better each year from 1920 through 1922. Despite those remarkable statistics, the Cleveland catcher has yet to be elected to the Hall of Fame. (National Baseball Hall of Fame Library, Cooperstown, N.Y.)

and one who was "still the same person as when he left home." "A boy who can keep his head after prosperity and the laudation of the nation's fans is indeed a man of great character," he added.[43]

After his playing career ended in 1928, O'Neill turned to managing, where he also experienced considerable success. He was a low-key pilot who quickly gained a reputation as a developer of players, many of whom became Hall of Famers. Nor did the Minooka native ever suffer a losing season in 14 years at the helm. As manager of Cleveland from 1935 to 1937, he made a shortstop out of Lou Boudreau and guided a young Bob Feller toward stardom. At Detroit, where he managed from 1943 to 1948, he taught the volatile Hal Newhouser how to focus on winning instead of arguing with umpires and captured his only World Series in 1945.[44] Moving on to the Philadelphia Phillies in the 1950s, O'Neill nurtured another Hall of Fame pitcher. "Steve was the greatest manager I'd ever known," said Robin Roberts, shortly after his induction at Cooperstown. "Between innings, he'd practically take the game apart. He'd call every pitch and by listening to him, he made a smarter and better pitcher out of me."[45]

That Steve O'Neill does not have a bronze plaque in the National Baseball Hall of Fame is a tragic oversight by the Baseball Writers, and one that will hopefully be rectified by the Veterans Committee sometime in the near future.

Though not a Hall of Famer either, Jack Quinn enjoyed the most unique career of any anthracite product. A spitballer who pitched for eight teams (New York Yankees, Boston Braves, Baltimore, Chicago White Sox, Boston Red Sox, Philadelphia A's, Brooklyn Dodgers, and Cincinnati Reds) in three major leagues (American, Federal and National) during four different decades (1909–1933), the Hazleton native made his final appearance at age 50.[46] He was also known to create his own legend by fabricating key events in his major league career, including his debut with the New York Yankees.[47]

Quinn made his debut on April 15, 1909, against the Washington Senators. He claims to have opposed "the great Walter Johnson, one of the fastest pitchers in the history of the game." "About the middle innings, it suddenly dawned on me that Washington hadn't scored and that I was pitching a shut out," he explained. "So I began mixing up curves and using the change of pace, and from then on the Senators ceased hitting." Quinn allegedly earned his first major league shutout that day, 3-0, leading him to conclude that "Johnson wasn't the greatest pitcher in the game, but that [he] was."[48] The *New York Times*, however, reported that Quinn's pitched against Bob Groom in his debut — not Johnson — and that Washington scored one run off the Yankee hurler, the final score being 4-1.[49] Nevertheless, Quinn continued to insist that the "courage, confidence and

Jack Quinn of Hazleton pitched for eight different major league clubs during the four different decades, making his final appearance at the age of 50 for the Cincinnati Reds. (National Baseball Hall of Fame Library, Cooperstown, N.Y.)

determination I gained by beating Johnson carried me through so many years of baseball."[50]

The cocky spitballer jumped to Baltimore of the Federal League in 1914, where he experienced the best and worst seasons of his career. In 1914 he posted a 26-14 record, and the following season went 9-22. After three years in the Pacific Coast League, he returned to the majors with the Chicago White Sox in 1918, but an ongoing feud with owner Charles Comiskey resulted in the sale of his contract to the Yankees.[51] There he appeared both as a starter and reliever, helping the Yankees to their first pennant in 1921. The Philadelphia Athletics purchased the 41-year-old hurler in 1925. Used almost exclusively as a reliever, Quinn's remarkable control and low-breaking spitball were major assets for a young pitching staff that would help the A's to a championship dynasty between 1929 and 1931. After being knocked out of Game Four of the 1929 World Series, Quinn became the object of the sportswriters' derision. Some, like John Debringer of the *New York Times*, wrote his obituary, reporting that the "pitching Methuselah's forty odd years caused him to collapse" and that his once-effective spitball was "badly shattered."[52]

But Quinn defied his critics and pitched in the majors for another four years. The secret to his success was a year-round conditioning program. During the off-season, he returned to his hunting lodge in Sunbury where he engaged in trap shooting — something he believed kept his eyes sharp. He also did a lot of walking since he believed that a pitcher "places almost as much strain on his legs during a game as he does on his throwing arm." Each afternoon, he would stand in front of a mirror and pantomine his pitching motion for an hour, believing that the exercise would allow him to keep his shoulder and arm ligaments "oiled up" and prevent the "inevitable stiffness that set in after a strenuous season."[53] It paid off. Quinn set records as the oldest player to win a major league game (49) to start a World Series game (46), finish a World Series game (47) and lead in a major pitching category (49) with six saves in 1932. A teammate of 31 Hall of Famers, he probably would have others believe he belonged in Cooperstown, too.[54]

Joe Boley was one of Quinn's teammates on Connie Mack's championship dynasty of 1929–31, which captured two World Series and three American League pennants over that span. With first baseman Jimmie Foxx, second baseman Max Bishop, and third baseman Jimmy Dykes, Boley formed one of the greatest infields in the game's history. Though he did hit with the power of teammates Foxx, Michey Cochrane or Al Simmons, he was an exceptional fielder. "Joe did have a very strong arm," according to Bing Miller, who played right field for the A's during those championship years. "But he could get the ball away in a hurry. With that and the start he made to get the ball, he could throw out even the fastest runners. He also took great pride in judging hitters. No one ever hit a ball in back of him, unless he was crossed up by the pitcher. That's why he could field balls near second base that normally went for hits."[55]

Boley was sold to Cleveland in 1932 when Mack began breaking up the championship dynasty. He ended his major league career that same season with a lifetime batting average of .269 and a fielding average of .957 in 538 games.[56]

The 1940s and 1950s brought many changes to baseball. After weathering the Great Depression the game was totally disrupted by the Second World War. Major league rosters were stripped of their star players by the draft and as the largely male baseball public declined in numbers, so did attendance at the games. Consequently, several teams found themselves in financial straits.[57] But baseball rebounded during the post-war years with an increasing exposure to new audiences. Night games, which were introduced in the 1930s, became accepted practice with the installation of arc lights at ballparks. Regular radio broadcasts continued to promote the game and add a new source of income. But the most profound change came with the introduction of the television in the 1950s. Teams that had once depended largely on the support of the home city now found themselves competing for a national audience. Not only did TV stimulate new interest in baseball throughout the country, especially in areas where there were no major league teams, but it also freed the clubs from total financial dependence on ticket sales.[58] For the baseball prodigies of northeastern Pennsylvania, all of these changes resulted in greater exposure for them and, in some cases, allowed them to make the major leagues. Pete Gray was among the greatest beneficiaries.

Baseball historians have credited the one-armed outfielder's single season in the majors to the depletion of quality players during World War II. Some maintain that the St. Louis Browns, "hungry for attendance, bought Gray partly as a gate attraction." Others view him solely as a "curiosity item" who "got his chance because of all the missing players who had gone off to war."[59] While the war years did, indeed, create a void that allowed Gray to crack the majors, it would be wrong to ignore the ability, courage, and perseverance he demonstrated with the Browns in 1945.

At spring training, Gray provided his teammates and management with some favorable first impressions. During his initial batting practices he began driving balls into the outfield as if he had been hitting all winter. He was just as impressive shagging fly balls, and the younger fans soon flocked to imitate his one-handed style. More importantly, while he simply wanted to be judged on the merits of his ability, Gray understood the controversy surrounding his promotion and how it connected to the need for higher gate receipts. Accordingly, he was careful not to jeopardize his personal integrity or the goodwill of management in his remarks to the press. When asked to make predictions about his performance in the big leagues, the one-armed outfielder responded diplomatically: "I surely am going to give it everything I have. I want to make good, not only for myself, but for the Browns. I hope I can make a lot of money for them, for they are willing to give me my big chance. I know I've got to make good to be an attraction, but I do know thousands of people are rooting for me. A lot of them are servicemen. They'll be watching to see what I do in the box scores, and if I make the team, there will be a lot of them out to see me play."[60]

On May 20, 1945, Pete Gray, the "One-Armed Wonder" of the St. Louis Browns, achieved his boyhood dream of playing at New York's Yankee Stadium. Playing both ends of a doubleheader in centerfield, Gray went 4-for-4, knocked in 2 runs and fielded his position flawlessly as the Browns swept the Bronx Bombers, 10-1 and 5-2. (Courtesy of Pete Gray.)

Although Gray insisted that he did not expect any special favors, Manager Luke Sewell made it clear that he wasn't planning to offer any. Sewell had retained the starting lineup of his 1944 pennant-winning team, and he believed that it was strong enough to repeat in 1945. If Gray could contribute to the team's success, Sewell would find a place in the line-up for him. But he admitted that he regarded the one-armed outfielder as "just another ball player."[61]

Gray's first opportunity came against the Detroit Tigers in the Browns' home opener. Facing Hal Newhouser, a future Hall of Famer, he singled up the middle, removing any doubt about his ability to hit major league pitching. By May, Gray was the Browns' lead-off hitter and played either left or center field.[62] Then, on May 20, the Nanticoke native realized his boyhood dream of playing in Yankee Stadium. A crowd of 36,000 packed the House that Ruth Built to watch a doubleheader between the Yankees and the Browns. Among them was an entourage from the Nanticoke area, including Gray's parents. He wouldn't let them down.

Playing center field and leading off, Gray, in his first at-bat, lined a fast ball to right field for the first hit of Game One. During his second trip to the plate, Yankee pitcher Spud Chandler challenged him with another fast ball on the first pitch. Once again, Gray hit a line-drive single to right. Infuriated that he had been shown-up by a one-armed rookie, Chandler responded like a mad bull, kicking the mound in frustration. By the end of the afternoon, Gray had reached base five times with four hits and knocked in two runs while fielding his position flawlessly in nine chances. The Browns swept the doubleheader 10-1 and 5-2.[63]

"The only thing I ever wanted to do as a kid was to play in Yankee Stadium," Gray recalled years later. "I had always been a big Yankee fan growing up and Babe Ruth was my hero. In fact, after he called his own home run during the 1932 World Series, I said to myself, 'Pete, the whole trick is confidence in yourself. If you are sure you can do it, you will do it.' And on May 20, 1945, it happened. My dream came true. Not only that, but I went 4 for 5. It can't get any better than that!"[64]

Although Gray weighed only 150 pounds, his left arm was so power-ful that it could wield a 36-ounce bat — heavier than those used by most major league hitters at the time. Realizing that the one-armed rookie had to begin his swing early to compensate for his handicap, pitchers tried to take advantage of him by blowing fast balls by him. But Gray's superb eye and good bat control enabled him to excel as a fast-ball hitter, though he does admit to having trouble with breaking balls. "Had I been thrown nothing but fast balls, I would've been a .300 hitter in the majors. But when the pitchers discovered that I couldn't hit the slower breaking balls, they fed me a steady diet of curves."[65]

Unfortunately, Gray was unable to sustain his remarkable early per-formance and ended up appearing in only 77 games for the 1945 Browns, who finished in third place. His major league career was destined to end on V-J day when many of the game's stars returned from the battlefront. Though he completed the season with a .218 average, he did manage to collect 51 hits— 43 singles, 6 doubles and 2 triples— draw 13 walks, and struck out just 11 times.[66] Those are remarkable statistics for a one-armed player, whose example inspired many servicemen who returned home from the war as amputees. World War II might have helped Pete Gray crack the majors, but there is no question that it made him an American hero.

Harry Dorish of Swoyersville made his major league pitching debut two years later on April 15, 1947, with the Boston Red Sox. On that day, he chalked up the first of seven victories he would post that season. "That first big league win was quite a thrill for me," he admitted. " I was playing with stars like Ted Williams, Vern Stephens, Birdie Tebbitts, Bobby Doerr and Dom DiMaggio. We were a pennant-contending team. In fact, everything that first year in the majors was just such a thrill for me. I roomed with

Williams, who was a first-class person. Got a real education from his tremendous knowledge of hitting."[67] The Red Sox would go on to finish in third place that season, following it up with two second-place finishes in 1948 and 1949. Dorish was used sparingly during those two seasons and afterward became a journeyman relief pitcher.

Over the next seven years he pitched for the St. Louis Browns, Chicago White Sox and Baltimore Orioles, completing his career in 1956 with a total record of 45-43, 332 strikeouts and a 3.83 ERA.[68] "I worked hard to make it to the majors," he said years later, reflecting on his baseball career, "and I worked harder to stay up there. But no regrets. I had the chance to rub elbows with some of the greatest players in the history of the game."[69]

Like Dorish, the other northeastern Pennsylvanians who played in the majors during the 1950s were simply grate-

Harry Dorish of Swoyersville admits that he "worked hard to make the majors" and "worked harder to stay up there," which he managed to do for seven years as a teammate of such greats as Ted Williams, Bobb Doerr, and Birdie Tebbitts. (National Baseball Hall of Fame Library, Cooperstown, N.Y.)

ful for having had that experience, regardless of the length of their stay in the majors and whether or not they were with a contending team. Joe Ostrowski, for example, realized a boyhood dream when he was traded to the New York Yankees in 1950. A control pitcher who began his major league career with the St. Louis Browns, Ostrowski filled the Yankees' void for a left-handed reliever, something they needed to contend. He arrived in New York in mid-season and found himself on the same team with Joe DiMaggio, Billy Martin, Whitey Ford and Allie Reynolds. "You know, all of those men were not only super ballplayers, but real gentlemen too," he remembered. "It was part of the Yankee tradition. We were expected to conduct ourselves, both on and off the field, in a manner that reflected well on the organization."[70]

Harry Dorish (left) poses with Mickey Mantle and a young fan and his Boston Red Sox roommate Ted Williams before a game at Yankee Stadium. (Courtesy of Mrs. Harry Dorish.)

In his first season with New York, Ostrowski went 1-1 with 3 saves and a 3.65 ERA. The following season he went 6-4 and collected five saves for the Bronx Bombers, helping them to another American League pennant.[71] He also pitched in his first and only World Series. Nicknamed the "professor" by his Yankee teammates because of his scholarly manner and off-season employment as a teacher at West Wyoming High School, Ostrowski faced the meat of the New York Giants' batting order — Willie Mays, Whitey Lockman and Wes Westrum. "I retired Mays on a fly ball to center, struck out Lockman and gave up a base hit to Westrum before I was pulled," he said. "I'd have to say, though, that signing my name to a Yankee contract was a dream come true. Never made more than $8,500, but it didn't matter. Any time I put that uniform on and got into a game, that was a highlight for me."[72] Ostrowski completed his five-year major league career with New York in 1952, retiring with a 23-25 career record, 131 strikeouts and 15 saves.[73]

Only two Yankees hold the honor of being nicknamed the "Professor"—Casey Stengel and West Wyoming's Joe Ostrowski, who earned the title because of his scholarly appearance and off-season profession as a school teacher. Ostrowski appeared in the 1951 World Series and rubbed elbows with such Yankee greats as Mickey Mantle, Billy Martin and Joe DiMaggio. (Courtesy of Joe Ostrowski.)

Stan Pawloski, on the other hand, modestly reminds anyone who asks him about his major league experience that he was "only up for a cup of coffee." The Wanamie native came up through the Cleveland organization, which contended for the American League pennant in 1951, 1952 and 1953 and finally captured the flag in 1954. The Indians opened the 1955 campaign

A control pitcher for the 1950–52 New York Yankees, Joe Ostrowski (right) was a teammate of the great "Yankee Clipper," Joe DiMaggio, who he considered not only a "super ballplayer" but a "real gentleman" as well. (Courtesy of Joe Ostrowski.)

with the oldest roster in all of major league baseball, the average age being 33 years old. A decision was made to integrate some of their younger minor league talent with the established stars in the hope that the team would continue to contend. Pawloski, who played shortstop and second base, was one of seven farmhands called up by the Tribe, but unfortunately there was no place for him in the infield. With star players like Bobby Avila, George Strickland and Al Rosen still in their prime, he saw action in only two games. He went 1 for 8, his only major league hit coming off of Paul Foytack of the Detroit Tigers.

Invited to spring training in 1956, Pawloski gave an outstanding performance at second base. Rosen, an exceptional power hitter but not much of a fielder, was so impressed he told the youngster, "If I could field like you, I'd be making $100,000 in this game!" But at the end of camp, Pawloski was sent back to Triple-A Indianapolis with the promise that "if something happens to Avila or Rosen, you'll be called right up."[74] It never happened, but there were no regrets.

"Just being in the majors was a real thrill for me," he admitted, reflecting on the experience years later. "I remember standing on the field at Comiskey Park in Chicago listening to the national anthem. I thought back to my childhood, about my parents, and about how grateful I was to them for giving me the opportunity to be in that ballpark on a beautiful, star-lit, summer night. Being grateful that the Cleveland Indians were actually paying me to play a kid's game, a game I loved from the first time I can remember."[75]

Steve Bilko of Nanticoke was given a much greater opportunity in the majors than Pawloski, but the slugger was never able to produce the same kind of phenomenal numbers that impressed so many in the minors. First called up in 1949 by the St. Louis Cardinals, Bilko didn't last the full season. He wouldn't see the majors again until 1953, when he became the

Cards' regular first baseman. He hit .251 that season and also enjoyed career highs in home runs (21), RBI (84), runs (72) and walks (70). But his 125 strikeouts also limited his productivity and he never played regularly again.[76] By the end of his 10-year major league career, Bilko had played for five different teams—the Cardinals, Chicago Cubs, Cincinnati Reds, Los Angeles Angels, and Detroit Tigers—and had compiled a .249 batting average, 76 home runs, and 276 RBI.[77]

Another Cardinal prospect was Bob Duliba of Glen Lyon. The 5'10", 175-pound pitcher was called up to St. Louis along with Hall of Famer Bob Gibson in 1959. "We got along pretty well, being in the same boat," Duliba recalled. "Gibby called me 'Sarge,' just being out of the Marines. We came up together as starting pitchers in the Cards' organization. But the real thrill for me was just being around Stan Musial and seeing him get his 3,000th hit. He was such a down-to-earth kind of guy, a real team player. Very unassuming. He'd talk to *everybody* on the team, no matter if you were a rookie or a veteran."[78]

When he got to the majors, Duliba was converted into a reliever. A control pitcher with an effective sinker, he appeared in 66 games over the course of two and a half seasons with the Cards, compiling a 3.01 ERA.[79] Of the six victories the Glen Lyon native collected, the first and most memorable came against Sandy Koufax of the Dodgers.

Traded to the Los Angeles Angels in 1963, Duliba enjoyed his best season the following year going 6-4 with nine saves and a 3.59 ERA. His swan song came in 1967 with Charlie Finley's Kansas City Athletics. Finley was among the greatest—and most controversial—promoters in the history of the game. "You name it, he did everything," said Duliba.

A phenomenal power hitter as well as a celebrity in the Pacific Coast League, Steve Bilko enjoyed his best seasons in the majors with the St. Louis Cardinals. He was also the inspiration of the 1950s television sit-com "Sergeant Bilko," starring Phil Silvers. (National Baseball Hall of Fame Library, Cooperstown, N.Y.)

"He had different colored uniforms, sox, jackets and even shoes. We played one exhibition game against the Dodgers that year and not one player on our team had the same uniform. There were guys with green sox, and others with gold sox. Some had gold shirts on, other had white shirts. It was crazy. But I'll tell you, I am grateful to Finley because he did me a favor. I was pitching in the minors in 1969 and I only needed 19 days of service to qualify for a major league pension. He gave me those 19 days. Paid all my expenses. For that I will always be grateful to him."[80] At the end of his major league career, Duliba had compiled a 17-12 record, 14 saves, 129 strikeouts and a 3.47 ERA.[81]

Joe Paparella of Eynon almost turned down the opportunity to go to the majors, but ultimately enjoyed two decades as an American League umpire. "When I was in the American Association I didn't worry a bit about my ability to make the grade," he recalled. "But I had some misgivings about the final hurdle. I didn't want to be left behind to grow old at that level as some had been made to do. That's why I informed the league president George Trautman after the 1945 season that I had decided to quit." Fortunately, Trautman refused to accept his resignation and sent him on to the American League in 1946.[82]

Once in the majors, Paparella was mentored by the legendary Cal Hubbard. Considered one of the greatest baseball minds in the game, Hubbard's imposing 6'3", 250-pound size and 20-10 eyesight made him one of the best at his trade. "Often, when he was the dean of our

Bob Duliba of Glen Lyon came up through the St. Louis Cardinals farm system as a prospective starting pitcher, along with Hall of Famer Bob Gibson. Converted into a reliever, Duliba appeared in 66 games during his three seasons with the Cards, compiling a 3.01 ERA and chalked up his most memorable win against Dodgers great Sandy Koufax. (National Baseball Hall of Fame Library, Cooperstown, N.Y.)

crew we would sit in our dressing room two hours after a game, breaking down an unusual play," Paparella said of the Hall of Fame umpire. "He had a fatherly approach, soft and kind, although big and gruff when challenged. He never tore down anyone and I am indebted beyond words for the manner in which he instilled confidence in me. It was not unusual, for example, for Cal to come to your room after a particularly trying game and spend hours restoring your belief in yourself, so that you could walk on the diamond the next day, head held high."[83] Paparella learned well.

When he became the American League's senior umpire in 1963, Paparella followed Hubbard's example. On the field, he was careful to hustle and always patient to listen to a reasonable complaint, but quick to act firmly if a player threatened to become physically abusive or used profanity.[84] Above all he was fair. When asked if Yankee great, Mickey Mantle was a "crybaby," as so many other umpires claimed, Paparella replied: "No, Mickey might have questioned a pitch, but he did it in such a way that no one in the stands knew he was doing it. I had no problem with that." In his estimation, though, Ted Williams had the best approach. "He was a champ," said Paparella of the last .400 hitter. "If you missed a pitch and Ted had the radar eyes to detect it, he never protested. But the next time at bat he might say, 'Didn't you think that pitch was low, or outside?' depending on where it was. But Williams was a class act. Where you run into trouble is with the mediocre hitters who think the world is against them and will try to convince you that they are better than their ability indicates by crying for justice."[85]

Paparella also demonstrated great trust and respect for the umpires on his crew, at times at his own expense. Once, while working behind the plate at Boston's Fenway Park, Paparella was unaware that his first base umpire had called "time" and subsequently allowed Detroit's pitcher to register two strikes on the Red Sox batter. After the matter was brought to his attention, the anthracite arbiter found himself in the embarrassing situation of having to cancel the two strikes. But he accepted his responsibility without excuse.[86] Off the field, Paparella demonstrated the same patience and fatherly approach to his younger colleagues as his own mentor. Often, he would sit for hours after a game and discuss it with them, or after a particularly hard contest be there to offer his support.

When he retired after the 1965 season, Paparella had the distinction of having called four World Series and four All Star Games. But he had also earned an enduring nickname, given to him by the younger umpires in his crew ... "Pappy."

In reviewing the major league experiences of the 21 anthracite products, there are three personal traits that become apparent, regardless of the length or success of their careers. Chief among those qualities is genuine humility grounded in a sense of gratitude for simply having made it to the big leagues. There was a common realization among the men that by cracking the majors each one had made it to the top of their chosen profession. And they were thankful simply for having been given the opportunity, by their parents, the coaches who helped them along the way, and the organization that took a chance on them.

Second, is the remarkable work ethic that got them to the majors and, in many cases, kept them there. When given the opportunity to play, they seized it, refusing to take a break, even if they had to endure a painful injury. "Hustle," "perseverance," and "heart" were more than words to them; they were values at the core of a unyielding work ethic that was instilled in the anthracite culture of northeastern Pennsylvania.

Finally, there was a common dedication to "fair play," whether it be in demanding the kind of salary they had rightfully earned, or playing by the rules, both on and off the field. While their childhoods taught them that the world can be a harsh place, there was no reason to compromise one's integrity in order to get ahead. Whether it was inspired by personal experience or religious conviction, these men believed that wrongful behavior could only breed misfortune.

If nothing else, these three traits defined them as men of character, who forged a special legacy in the major leagues as "diamonds from the coalfields."

7

Quittin' Time

Beginning in the late 1940s, the anthracite industry spiraled into a steady decline. With the growth of the oil and electrical industries, America was no longer dependent on the black diamond. Mine employment fell from 80,000 to less than half that number a decade later. With little opportunity for work, out-migration increased. The young left first, followed by middle-aged heads of families. By 1960, the anthracite region had the lowest per capita income in Pennsylvania and unemployment compensation was the major source of income in the region's largest cities of Scranton and Wilkes-Barre. In the small towns, which once formed the heart of the coal industry, the elderly were left to subsist on social security and welfare checks or money sent back home by their sons and daughters working elsewhere.[1] The kingdom of coal was gone, and so was the golden age of baseball.

Like coal miners too old to make a new start, many of the major leaguers returned to northeastern Pennsylvania after their playing days had ended to deal with the sense of loss, sadness and sometimes anger that followed. Some were able to come to terms with those feelings and find a new meaning in family and friends. Others still kept one foot in the past and one in the present, living in the reflected glory of their days in the majors or by returning to the professional ranks to manage.

To be sure, there are some tragedies among Pennsylvania's anthracite baseball players. Christy Mathewson's story is the most poignant. Returning

After his playing career ended, Mathewson (right) rejoined his old manager and friend John McGraw as a coach for the New York Giants. But the constant bouts of coughing and recurring fever he suffered, the result of tuberculosis, left him drained, and he was forced to retire after just one season. (National Baseball Hall of Fame Library, Cooperstown, N.Y.)

home from World War I where he was exposed to poison gas, Matty contracted what appeared to be a lingering cold. It was, in fact, an advanced case of tuberculosis, the same illness that claimed his younger brother Harry's life at the age of 31.[2] Mathewson rejoined the New York Giants in 1919 as a coach, but most of the time he was subdued and fatigued. His constant bouts of coughing, recurring fever and diminished appetite resulted in considerable weight loss. His once-handsome face became pasty, the deep blue color in his eyes lost their glow, and the 6'1", 195-pound frame which once dominated opposing batters appeared shrunken. He retired to his five-bedroom colonial home in the Highland Park section of Saranac Lake in upstate New York where he began to recuperate. Once again, in 1923, he tried to return to the game as president of the Boston Braves and, once again, his illness got the better of him and he returned to Saranac Lake.[3]

On the morning of October 7, 1925, Matty, consumed by fever and barely able to talk, called his wife Jane to his bedside and told her: "It is nearly over. I know it and we must face it. Go out and have a good cry. Don't make it a long one. This is something we can't help."[4] Later that day, he died, at the age of 45.

Mathewson's death caused tremendous sadness across the nation. He was eulogized in prose and poetry in major newspapers, becoming larger than life itself. Grantland Rice, New York's legendary baseball writer, wrote that Matty's "spirit and inspiration was greater than his game" and that he was "one of those rare characters who appealed to the millions through a magnetic personality, attached to a clean, honest and undying loyalty to a cause."[5] Among the most moving epitaphs was the following poem, by Leo F. Gleason, which appeared in the *Philadelphia Inquirer*.

"Matty"

Incomparable, he stands alone,
The paladin of the pitching hill.
When shall his genius ere be met,
How can another match his skill?

We shall miss him forever, his magic,
The sweep and thrill of his play;
For the mighty master hath vanished,
He fades from the firing today.

Across the mist and vale of time,
No more thrilling phrase, no pen, no science
Can conjure dreams of haunting lore,
Than 'Matty pitching for the Giants.'

He played his game so cleanly right,
He played it as it should be played.

No other star can hope to leave,
Such a wealth of greatness at the grave.

The 'greatest of pitchers,' ah, more than that,
A tradition true and noble in life.
Matty has passed to that greater game,
Where surely his star will be as bright.

Yes, down the roads and hills of years,
More stirring words, what mind could court?
To thrill the soul with joys and tears,
Than 'Mathewson pitching for New York.'

Inducted posthumously into the Hall of Fame in 1936, Mathewson continues to capture the imagination of the sporting world three-quarters of a century after his death. His biographer Ray Robinson has convincingly argued that the legendary pitcher allowed the game of baseball to spin off into the larger culture by having his likeness appear on advertisements as well as baseball cards. His example as a gentleman-athlete transcended the game and set a standard for later stars in other sports. In the process, Matty became the very first American sports hero.[7] His legend

Mathewson the father with his only child, son Christy, Jr., who would also die tragically at a young age. (National Baseball Hall of Fame Library, Cooperstown, N.Y.)

continues to fascinate younger generations of sports fans who read Eric Rolfe Greenberg's *The Celebrant*, considered to be the finest baseball novel ever written.[8]

In northeastern Pennsylvania, Matty holds a special status as a native son. At Factoryville, where he was born and raised, there is a bronze statue erected in his honor. At Keystone College, where he attended prep school, an archives contains personal items from his playing days, including major league contracts, the black flannel uniform he wore in 1912, his army uniform from World War I, scrapbooks full of clippings from his career, and an especially moving photo of him and his only son, Christy Jr., who was later killed in a gas explosion at the young age of 44.[9] Bucknell University, where Mathewson attended college, also has an archives containing many items from his collegiate career, as well as a football stadium dedicated in his honor.[10] He is also buried in the small college town, in a grave overlooking the green fields of the Bucknell campus. It was, after all, in Lewisburg, in a small home on Market Street, where he spent some of the happiest years of his life.[11]

Jake Daubert also died at an early age. After completing the 1924 season with the Cincinnati Reds, Daubert began making plans to purchase the Reading, Pennsylvania, club. He hoped to play one more year in the majors, and then retire to a managerial position with the International League club.[12] But complications from an appendectomy developed and he died, unexpectedly, on October 9 at the age of 40.[13] For others, the tragedy came from addictive behavior.

Pete Gray, for example, struggled with alcoholism and gambling, being left to wonder if he had, in fact, been promoted to the majors as a curiosity item rather than for his baseball ability. After the 1945 season, the St. Louis Browns sold his contract to the Toledo Mud Hens. In 1946 he appeared in only 48 games for Toledo, hitting just .250. Gray sat out the 1947 season, returning to pro ball with the Class A Elmira Pioneers in 1948. Being the oldest player on a club that was rebuilding, he battled a strained hamstring that limited his playing time. The 78 hits, 14 RBI and .290 average he compiled that season would have been a promising sign for most minor leaguers, but at the age of 33, it was a last blaze of glory for the one-armed outfielder. He would end his professional baseball career the next season as a reserve outfielder for Dallas of the Texas League.[14]

Since his one year in the major leagues did not qualify him for a pension, Gray managed to earn a modest income by returning to Nanticoke, where he opened a pool hall and rented out rooms in the same white, double-block house his family built at the turn of the 19th century. He also continued to battle alcoholism and a severe gambling addiction for many years, but managed to recover from both.[15]

Pete Gray visits with some of his admirers: the author, his nephew and his two young sons. (Author's collection.)

Though Gray shunned the spotlight, he did agree to have his life's story told in film and book.[16] An inspirational made-for-television movie, *A Winner Never Quits*, was filmed in 1986, starring actor Keith Carradine. It is still shown on many of the major TV networks across the nation each spring on the eve of the baseball season.[17] Shortly after, I began my research on a book about his life titled *One-Armed Wonder: Pete Gray, Wartime Baseball and the American Dream*. Published in 1995, the book has become rather popular in the Wyoming Valley of northeastern Pennsylvania and continues to introduce the members of a younger generation to a ballplayer who inspired the nation during World War II.[18] Today, Gray resides at a Nanticoke nursing home, greeting family, friends and, on occasion, school children who come to visit him.

Jack Quinn also struggled with alcoholism. Released by the Cincinnati Reds in 1933 shortly after his 49th birthday, he pitched a few games for Hollywood of the Pacific Coast League the following season before returning to Pennsylvania where he managed briefly for Johnstown of the Mid-Atlantic League. After his wife, Georgiana, died in 1940, Quinn was left alone. He moved back to the Pottsville area where he spent his time at a local bar pitching pennies, talking sports and drinking to excess. In January 1946, he entered Good Samaritan Hospital, in an attempt to recover. He died there in April of the same year and is buried next to his wife in the Charles Baber Cemetery in Pottsville.[19]

Steve Bilko's major league career was afflicted by an eating disorder. In good seasons he maintained his weight at 230 pounds and promised to get down to 200 pounds in the off-season. Instead, he would report to spring training even heavier and struggle to get back to the 230 weight.[20] Sadly, Bilko would earn the reputation among sportswriters of a "fat guy who would swing at anything" and a first baseman who would "stand rooted at the bag as ground balls skittered into the outfield."[21] It was cruel as well as unfair to a man who had become a celebrity in the Pacific Coast League just as much for his remarkable power hitting as for his dedication to the fans, especially youngsters. Bilko had his own "army" of admirers in Los Angeles. They came to see him play and sat along the right field line to cheer their hero, who could be found before and after the game signing autographs or offering a word of encouragement to aspiring major leaguers. There was even a popular 1950s sitcom called "Sergeant Bilko," which was inspired by the Nanticoke native. Retiring from the game in 1962, Bilko, who was offered a plethora of jobs in the Los Angeles area, chose to return to northeastern Pennsylvania. His decision was based on family, and a strong desire to raise his children in the same community where he had grown up. He took a job as a sales representative for the Dana Perfume company in Wilkes-Barre, where he died at the age of 49 in 1978.[22]

Other anthracite products found their niche as managers after their playing days ended. Among those to enjoy success at the major league level was Hughie Jennings, who led the Detroit Tigers to pennants during his first three years at the helm, 1907–09. In 1920, the Pittston native briefly left the game to practice law with his brother in Scranton, but the retirement was short lived. The following season, he joined his long-time friend, John McGraw, as an assistant coach of the New York Giants. He quickly became an idol at the Polo Grounds, where his antics and war cries from the coaching box endeared him to players and fans alike.[23]

In 1925, Jennings, his health failing from tuberculosis, was forced to retire for good. He entered a sanitarium at Asheville, North Carolina, for treatment and appeared to recuperate enough to return to Scranton where he appeared in a court case in January 1928.[24] It proved to be a last hurrah. Stricken with meningitis, Jennings was hospitalized and lapsed into a coma for nearly three days. Just before he died in February, a doctor came to his bedside to check on him. The Hall of Famer slowly opened his eyes, grinned, and whispered hoarsely: "At-a-boy, Doc!"[25] Jennings is buried in St. Catherine's cemetery in Moscow. He was posthumously inducted into the Hall of Fame in 1945.[26]

Steve O'Neill managed for fifteen seasons in the majors, winning a World Series with the Detroit Tigers in 1945. O'Neill quickly earned the respect and affection of his players wherever he managed, treating them like sons. According to former Phillies farm director Joe Reardon, the Minooka native "had a heart as big as a mountain, and when someone would make a mistake, he'd tell 'em, 'So what!' and explain that in his playing days the boners were bigger and more frequent. The players were positively crazy about Steve."[27] After being released by the Philadelphia Phillies in 1954, O'Neill retired from baseball. He died eight years later at the age of 69. He is buried at St. Joseph's cemetery in Minooka on a hillside overlooking the old playing field where he began his baseball career.[28]

Bucky Harris was another manager who was loved and admired by his players. After managing the Washington Senators for 18 seasons, he

In 1920, Hughie Jennings retired from baseball and returned to Scranton to practice law. But the following year, he accepted an offer from his former Oriole teammate John McGraw to coach the New York Giants. (National Baseball Hall of Fame Library, Cooperstown, N.Y.)

became skipper of the Tigers, Red Sox, Phillies and Yankees, for which he captured another pennant.[29] So admired was he in New York that when the Yankees dismissed Harris in 1948 after a close third-place finish, the players circulated a petition on his behalf.[30] It was unsuccessful, and Harris returned to Washington as a special scout for his beloved Senators until they moved to Texas after the 1971 season.[31]

Harris would live for another six years, but they were painful ones. He suffered from Parkinson's disease and was virtually immobilized in his final years by a calcium deposit in his right hip.[32] If there was any consolation to old age, it was learning that he had been elected to the Hall of Fame in 1975, two years before his death at the age of 81.[33]

Still others ended their playing careers back in the minor leagues. Ed Walsh was released by the Boston Braves in 1917 after posting a 0-1 record. Having been overworked throughout his career, his fast ball was gone and he was beleaguered by a chronically sore arm. But he still believed that he could win in the majors by relying on his spitball. He returned to the minors to prove the point, first with Milwaukee of the American Association in 1919 and the following year with Bridgeport of the Eastern League. Over the course of those two seasons, Walsh posted a 3-3 record, managing to throw only 43 innings. Those numbers made clear to him that his pitching days were over.

He tried to redirect his passion into coaching, initially with an independent minor league team in Oneonta, New York, then with the Chicago White Sox, and finally at the University of Notre Dame. None of those experiences panned out, though, and Walsh moved to Meriden,

Harry Dorish (right) poses with Hall of Famer Bob Feller of the Cleveland Indians at an Old Timer's Game in the 1970s. Dorish earned his very first major league victory against Feller in 1947. (Courtesy of Mrs. Harry Dorish.)

Connecticut, where he took a job as a milkman. His biggest thrill came in 1946 when the Veterans Committee voted him into the Hall of Fame. He died of cancer in 1959 at the age of 78.[34]

Buck Freeman completed his major league career with the Boston Red Sox in 1907 and returned to the anthracite region to manage the Scranton Miners of the Eastern League. In the 1920s, Freeman turned his attention to scouting for the St. Louis Browns, which he did until 1935 when he opened a pool hall near his Wilkes-Barre home.[35] Joe Boley played shortstop for Williamsport of the New York-Pennsylvania League before joining the Philadelphia Athletics scouting staff in 1948.[36] Mike Gazella managed at Ponca City, Ventura and Denver before rejoining the Yankees as a scout in the 1940s.[37] Joe Shaute attempted to resurrect his pitching career in the late 1930s, first with Scranton of the New York-Pennsylvania League and later with the Wilkes-Barre Barons of the Eastern League. When the comeback failed, he, too, turned to managing with Scranton. Retiring from the game in 1942, he entered local politics in Scranton.[38] Eddie Murphy also returned to the minors where he enjoyed some success. After leaving the White Sox in 1921, he signed with Columbus of the American Association where he hit .353 and captured the league's batting title. That performance caught the attention of the Pittsburgh Pirates who brought him back to the majors for one final hurrah in 1926. The following year, Murphy returned to the minors for good, playing for Rochester and later Montreal of the International League before turning his attention to managing the Stroudsburg Poconos.[39]

For still others, the end of their professional careers came abruptly and they chose to move on from baseball with their lives, dedicating their time to family and friends. Stan Coveleski moved to South Bend, Indiana, after his retirement in 1929, and opened a service station on the west side of town. There he gave hours of free pitching lessons to local youngsters, playing catch behind the garage. When he died in 1984, the city of South Bend dedicated a baseball stadium in his honor.[40] Nestor Chylak spent his retirement on the speaking circuit. As a member of the *Sports Illustrated* Speaker's Bureau, he visited little leaguers and corporate and veterans groups talking about the intangible lessons he learned during his years in baseball.[41] Joe Ostrowski returned to the Wilkes-Barre area and immersed himself in the lives of junior high and high school students as a history teacher and baseball coach.[42] Bob Duliba also returned to the anthracite region to raise a family and coach at the high school and college levels.[43] Stan Pawloski relocated to Philadelphia where he took a job with Penn Ventilator Corporation and spent his evenings and weekends sharing his love of sports with his own four children.[44] Joe Paparella did the same with his grandchildren after his umpiring days were over.[45]

Only four of the players are still alive today — Duliba, Gray, Ostrowski, and Pawloski. Some may have had regrets about their professional baseball careers, though none shared any with me. Because they played before free agency, they certainly would be justified if they felt cheated by today's wild escalation of player salaries. But they seem to have disciplined themselves to get on with life, having benefited from the more intangible lessons they learned during their playing days.

"Baseball taught me that life is a journey and that journey is often more fun than the ultimate goal," said Pawloski, who seemed to best summarize the feelings of the surviving players. "The beginning was fun because all of the players were striving for the same thing. But as we got closer to the majors, it was every man for himself. The major leaguers knew that you were after their job, and they certainly didn't treat you too well. But that's life, too. You've got to earn what you get."

"Playing 150 games a year also taught me the importance of consistency. Sometimes you have to play through pain. You also have to be accountable because the very next morning, people turn to the box scores to see what you've done. You go from a 'hero' to a 'bum' a lot. But even with all that, I wouldn't have traded my pro career for anything."[46]

That kind of exemplary attitude best reflects the legacy of these 21 "diamonds from the coalfields." Although they began life at a disadvantage, they still managed to make it to the top of their chosen profession. No one can ever take that away from them. They realized their dream. What's more, each and every one did it with a genuine sense of humility, an exceptional work ethic, and a lot of class.

I only wish there were more like them in the major leagues today.

Appendix: Major and Minor League Career Statistics of Players Profiled

Steven Thomas (Steve) Bilko

Born: November 13, 1928, at Nanticoke, PA. Died: March 7, 1978, at Wilkes-Barre, PA
Height: 6'1"; weight: 230; threw and batted right-handed.

Year	Club	League	Pos.	G	AB	R	H	2B	3B	HR	RBI	BA	PO	A	E	FA
1945	Allentown	Interstate	OF	1	1	0	1	0	0	0	1	.000				
1946	Salisbury	Eastern Shore	1B	122	441	73	121	28	4	12	90	.274				
1947	Winston-Salem	Carolina	1B	116	438	109	148	26	3	29	120	.338				
1948	Rochester	International	1B	12	41	5	6	1	0	0	3	.146				
	Lynchburg	Piedmont	1B	128	463	89	154	34	6	20	92	.333				
1949	Rochester	International	1B	139	503	101	156	32	5	34	125	.310				
	St. Louis	National	1B	6	17	3	5	2	0	0	2	.294	42	3	0	1.000
1950	St. Louis	National	1B	10	33	1	6	1	0	0	2	.182	81	7	1	.989
	Rochester	International	1B-2B	109	334	71	97	18	6	15	58	.290				
1951	Columbus	American Assn.	1B	26	74	13	21	2	0	1	6	.284				
	Rochester	International	1B	73	273	41	77	14	6	8	50	.282				
	St. Louis	National	1B	21	72	5	16	4	0	2	12	.222	170	13	3	.984
1952	Rochester	International	1B	82	286	55	92	22	5	12	55	.322				
	St. Louis	National	1B	20	72	7	19	6	1	1	6	.264	177	24	1	.995
1953	St. Louis	National	1B	154	570	72	143	23	3	21	84	.251	1446	124	15	.991
1954	St. Louis / Chicago	National	1B	55	106	12	24	8	1	4	13	.226	203	35	0	1.000
1955	Los Angeles	Pacific Coast	1B	168	622	105	204	35	3	37	124	.328				
1956	Los Angeles	Pacific Coast	1B	162	597	163	215	18	6	55	164	.360				
1957	Los Angeles	Pacific Coast	1B	158	536	111	161	22	1	56	140	.300				
1958	Cincinnati / Los Angeles	National	1B	78	188	25	44	5	4	11	35	.234	345	28	2	.995
1959	Spokane	Pacific Coast	1B	135	478	76	146	24	1	26	92	.305				
1960	Detroit	American	1B	78	222	20	46	11	2	9	25	.207	501	36	5	.991
1961	Los Angeles	American	1B/OF	114	294	49	82	16	1	20	59	.279	579	61	7	.989
1962	Los Angeles	American	1B	64	164	26	47	9	1	8	38	.287	371	28	2	.995
1963	Rochester	International	1B	101	261	41	68	17	1	8	37	.261				
Minor League Totals: 13 years			1B-2B	1533	5349	1053	1667	293	47	313	1157	.312	3915	359	36	.992
Major League Totals: 10 years			1B	600	1738	220	432	85	13	76	276	.249				.992

John Peter Bolinsky (Joe) Boley

Born: July 19, 1896, at Mahanoy City, PA. Died: December 30, 1962, at Mahanoy City, PA.
Height: 5'11"; weight: 170 lbs.; threw and batted right-handed.

Year	Club	League	Pos.	G	AB	R	H	2B	3B	HR	RBI	BA	PO	A	E	FA
1917	Harrisburg	Tri-State	SS-3B	33	127	6	31	—	—	—	—	.244	57	92	13	.920
1918	In Military Service															
1919	Baltimore	International	SS	137	505	69	152	19	2	1	—	.301	303	451	42	.947
1920	Baltimore	International	SS	143	543	90	167	30	14	3	—	.308	300	488	49	.941
1921	Baltimore	International	SS	152	590	103	187	37	21	5	98	.317	334	491	38	.956
1922	Baltimore	International	SS	151	562	106	193	34	13	11	104	.343	345	410	34	.957
1923	Baltimore	International	SS	160	615	110	188	29	12	9	—	.306	344	453	53	.938
1924	Baltimore	International	SS	157	574	91	167	32	9	4	90	.291	331	468	28	.966
1925	Baltimore	International	SS	152	573	89	189	37	10	13	117	.330	324	428	38	.952
1926	Baltimore	International	SS	145	526	110	161	24	8	19	—	.306	323	522	22	.975
1927	Philadelphia	American	SS	116	370	49	115	18	8	1	52	.311	182	318	26	.951
1928	Philadelphia	American	SS	132	425	49	112	20	3	0	49	.264	244	320	30	.949
1929	Philadelphia	American	SS / 3B	91	303	36	76	17	6	2	47	.251	162	229	15	.963
1930	Philadelphia	American	SS	121	420	41	116	22	2	4	55	.276	221	296	16	.970
1931	Philadelphia	American	SS / 2B	67	224	26	51	9	3	0	20	.228	102	150	12	.955
1932	Philadelphia / Cleveland	American	SS	11	38	2	8	2	0	0	4	.211	11	20	3	.912
1933	Williamsport	New York-Penna.	SS	18	53	6	15	2	0	0	3	.283	17	29	3	.939
Minor League Totals: 10 years			SS-3B	1248	4668	780	1450	—	—	—	—	.303	2678	3832	320	.949
Major League Totals: 6 years			SS/2B/3B	538	1780	203	478	88	22	7	227	.269	922	1333	102	.957

WORLD SERIES

Year	Club	League	Pos.	G	AB	R	H	2B	3B	HR	RBI	BA	PO	A	E	FA
1929	Philadelphia	American	SS	5	17	1	4	0	0	0	1	.235	4	13	0	1.000
1930	Philadelphia	American	SS	6	21	1	2	0	0	0	1	.095	9	13	1	.960
1931	Philadelphia	American	PH	1	1	0	0	0	0	0	0	.000	0	0	0	—
World Series Totals: 3 years			SS	12	39	2	6	0	0	0	2	.154	13	26	1	.975

Stanley (Stan) Coveleski

Born: July 13, 1889 at Shamokin, PA. Died: March 20, 1984 at South Bend, IN.
Height: 5'9"; weight: 178 lbs.; threw and batted right-handed; named to Hall of Fame in 1969.

Year	Club	League	G	IP	W	L	Pct.	H	R	ER	SO	BB	ERA
1908	Shamokin	Atlantic	12	—	6	2	.750	—	—	—	—	—	—
1909	Lancaster	Tri-State	43	272	23*	11	.676	225	84	—	78	68	—
1910	Lancaster	Tri-State	30	—	15	8	.652	—	—	—	—	—	—
1911	Lancaster	Tri-State	36	272	15	19+	.441	288	120	—	154	65	—
1912	Atlantic City	Tri-State	39	—	20	13	.606	—	—	—	—	—	—
1912	Philadelphia	American	5	21	2	1	.667	18	9	—	9	4	—
1913	Spokane	Northwest	48	316	17	20*	.459	300	140	—	197	95	—
1914	Spokane	Northwest	43	314	20	15	.571	269	109	—	214*	99	—
1915	Portland	Pacific Coast	64*	293	17	17	.500	279	123	87	171	82	2.67
1916	Cleveland	American	45	232	15	12	.556	247	100	88	76	58	3.41
1917	Cleveland	American	45	297	19	14	.576	202	78	60	133	94	1.81
1918	Cleveland	American	38	311	22	13	.629	261	90	63	87	76	1.82
1919	Cleveland	American	43	286	24	12	.667	286*	99	83	118	60	2.52
1920	Cleveland	American	41	315	24	14	.632	284	110	87	133*	65	2.49
1921	Cleveland	American	43	316	23	13	.639	341	137	118	99	84	3.36
1922	Cleveland	American	35	277	17	14	.548	292	120	102	98	64	3.31
1923	Cleveland	American	33	228	13	14	.481	251	98	70	54	42	2.76*
1924	Cleveland	American	37	240	15	16	.484	286	140	108	58	73	4.05
1925	Washington	American	32	241	20	5	.800*	230	86	76	58	73	2.84*
1926	Washington	American	36	245	14	11	.560	272	122	85	50	81	3.12
1927	Washington	American	5	14	2	1	.667	13	7	5	3	8	3.21
1928	New York	American	12	58	5	1	.833	72	41	37	5	20	5.74
Minor League Totals:	8 years		315	—	133	105	.582	—	—	—	—	—	—
Major League Totals:	14 years		450	3081	215	141	.604	3055	1237	982	981	802	2.88

WORLD SERIES RECORD

Year	Club	League	G	IP	W	L	Pct.	H	R	ER	SO	BB	ERA
1920	Cleveland	American	3	27	3	0	1.000	15	2	2	8	2	0.67
1925	Washington	American	2	14.1	0	2	.000	16	7	6	3	5	3.77
World Series Totals	2 years		5	41.1	3	2	.600	31	9	8	11	7	1.74

*Indicates league leader. +Indicates tied for league lead

Jacob Ellsworth (Jake) Daubert

Born: May 14, 1885, at Lewellyn, PA Died: October 9, 1924, at Cincinnati, OH
Height: 5'10"; weight: 160 lbs.; threw and batted left-handed.

Year	Club	League	Pos.	G	AB	R	H	2B	3B	HR	RBI	BA	PO	A	E	FA
1907	Kane	Interstate	1B	42	157	18	47	—	—	—	—	.299	433	26	7	.985
1907	Marion	Ohio-Penna.	1B	71	265	26	75	—	—	—	—	.283	709	40	8	.989
1908	Nashville	Southern	1B	138	473	49	124	12	11	6	—	.262	1331	17	15	.989
1909	Toledo	American Assoc.	1B	35	129	16	24	6	0	0	—	.186	371	23	7	.983
1909	Memphis	Southern	1B	81	283	35	89	11	2	0	—	.314	806	58	4	.995
1910	Brooklyn	National	1B	144	552	67	146	15	15	8	52	.264	1418	72	16	.989
1911	Brooklyn	National	1B	149	573	89	176	17	8	5	46	.307	1485	88	18	.989
1912	Brooklyn	National	1B	145	559	81	172	19	16	3	73	.308	1373	76	10	.993*
1913	Brooklyn	National	1B	139	508	76	178	17	7	2	46	.350*	1279	80	13	.991
1914	Brooklyn	National	1B	126	474	89	156	17	7	6	44	.329*	1097	48	8	.993
1915	Brooklyn	National	1B	150	544	62	164	21	8	2	42	.301	1441	102*	11	.993
1916	Brooklyn	National	1B	127	478	75	151	16	7	3	35	.316	1195	66	9	.993*
1917	Brooklyn	National	1B	125	468	59	122	4	4	2	30	.261	1188	82	12	.991
1918	Brooklyn	National	1B	108	396	50	122	12	15*	2	47	.308	1069	63	10	.991
1919	Cincinnati	National	1B	140+	537	79	148	10	12	2	42	.276	1437	80	17	.989
1920	Cincinnati	National	1B	142	553	97	168	28	13	4	48	.304	1358	63	15	.990
1921	Cincinnati	National	1B	136	516	69	158	18	12	2	64	.306	1290	78	10	.993
1922	Cincinnati	National	1B	156+	610	114	205	15	22*	12	66	.336	1652*	79	11	.994+
1923	Cincinnati	National	1B	125	500	63	146	27	10	2	54	.292	1224	77	9	.993
1924	Cincinnati	National	1B	102	405	47	114	14	9	1	31	.281	1128	74	12	.990
Minor League Totals: 5 years				367	1307	144	359	—	—	—	—	.269	3650	164	41	.988
Major League Totals: 15 years				2014	7673	1117	2326	250	165	56	720	.303	19634	1128	181	.991

WORLD SERIES RECORD

Year	Club	League	Pos.	G	AB	R	H	2B	3B	HR	RBI	BA	PO	A	E	FA
1916	Brooklyn	National	1B	4	17	1	3	0	1	0	0	.176	40	3	0	1.000
1919	Cincinnati	National	1B	8	29	4	7	0	1	0	1	.241	81	5	2	.977
World Series Totals: 2 years			1B	12	46	5	10	0	2	0	1	.217	121	8	2	.985

*Indicates league leader. +Indicates tied for league lead

Robert John (Bobby) Duliba

Born: January 9, 1936, at Glen Lyon, PA.

Height: 5'10"; weight: 185 lbs.; threw and batted right-handed.

Year	Club	League	G	IP	W	L	Pct.	H	R	ER	SO	BB	ERA
1952	Ozark	Alabama-Fla.	18	106	6	5	.667	94	55	43	67	69	3.65
1953	St. Joseph	Western	43	128	12	3	.680	111	63	46	71	59	3.23
1954	Peoria	Three-I	37	169	9	10	.471	187	114	94	80	64	5.01
1955	Allentown	Eastern	5	9	1		.500	10	8	7	5	4	7.00
1955	Peoria	Three-I	29	91	5	4	.667	95	63	54	68	30	5.34
		IN MILITARY SERVICE											
1959	Omaha	American Association	37	123	8	5	.615	120	57	42	83	57	3.07
1959	St. Louis	National	11	23	0	1	.000	19	7	7	14	12	2.74
1960	St. Louis	National	27	41	4	4	.500	49	20	19	23	16	4.17
1961	Charlestown	International	59	101	7	7	.500	96	45	39	72	44	3.48
1962	Atlanta	International	30	50	3	4	.471	39	24	21	47	21	3.78
1962	St. Louis	National	28	39	2	0	1.000	33	11	9	22	17	2.08
1963	Hawaii	Pacific Coast	53	96	6	5	.600	89	44	31	89	16	2.91
1963	Los Angeles	American	6	8	1	1	.500	3	1	1	4	6	1.13
1964	Los Angeles	American	58	73	6	4	.600	80	35	29	33	22	3.58
1965	Toronto	International	15	33	4	1	.636	22	4	4	22	6	1.09
1965	Boston	American	39	64	4	2	.667	60	31	27	27	22	3.80
1966	Toronto	International	4	10	0	0	.000	16	6	6	8	1	5.40
1966	Vancouver	Pacific Coast	44	66	7	1	.900	55	14	14	49	10	1.91
1967	Kansas City	American	7	10	0	0	.000	13	7	7	6	1	6.30
1967	Vancouver	Pacific Coast	30	51	6	3	.667	64	21	18	37	13	3.18
1968	Vancouver	Pacific Coast	39	69	3	5	.375	77	28	21	30	18	2.74
1969	Des Moines	American Association	35	66	6	4	.600	76	30	27	45	20	3.63
1970	Richmond	International	43	78	4	6	.400	73	29	22	57	18	2.54
Minor League Totals:	16 years		521	1246	87	64	.547	1224	605	489	830	450	3.62
Major League Totals:	7 years		176	257	17	12	.586	257	112	99	129	96	3.47

Harry (Fritz) Dorish

Born: July 13, 1921, at Swoyersville, PA. Died: December 30, 2000, at Kingston, PA.
Height: 5'11"; weight: 204 lbs.; threw and batted right-handed.

Year	Club	League	G	IP	W	L	Pct.	H	R	ER	SO	BB	ERA
1941	Canton	Mid-Atlantic	21	120	7	6	.538	119	58	43	88	50	3.23
1942	Scranton	Eastern	24	148	12	8	.600	113	43	34	76	49	2.07
1943–45		IN MILITARY SERVICE											
1946	Louisville	American Assn.	28	146	11	4	.733	128	58	51	76	47	3.14
1947	Boston	American	41	136	7	8	.467	149	80	71	50	54	4.70
1948	Boston	American	9	15	0	1	.000	18	13	9	5	6	5.65
1948	Birmingham	Southern Assn.	16	99	9	4	.692	102	43	38	51	25	3.45
1949	Boston	American	5	8	0	0	.000	7	2	2	5	1	2.25
1949	Louisville	American Assn.	15	90	3	3	.500	103	60	51	45	35	5.10
1950	St. Louis	American	29	109	4	9	.308	162	90	78	36	36	6.44
1951	Chicago	American	32	97	5	6	.455	101	50	38	29	31	3.53
1952	Chicago	American	39	91	8	4	.667	66	28	25	47	42	2.47
1953	Chicago	American	55	146	10	6	.625	140	59	55	69	52	3.39
1954	Chicago	American	37	109	6	4	.600	88	35	33	48	29	2.72
1955	Chicago/Baltimore	American	48	83	5	3	.625	74	29	26	28	37	2.82
1956	Baltimore/Boston	American	28	43	0	2	.000	45	20	18	15	13	3.86
1957	San Francisco	Pacific Coast	31	190	9	12	.429	207	87	70	70	59	3.32
1958	Minneapolis	American Assn.	48	93	3	3	.500	76	26	23	43	30	2.23
1959	Mineapolis / Houston	American Assn.	4	8	1	0	1.000	10	4	2	4	1	2.25
Minor League Totals:	8 years		187	894	55	40	.624	858	379	312	453	296	3.09
Major League Totals:	10 years		323	835	45	43	.511	850	406	355	332	301	3.83

John F. (Buck) Freeman

Born: October 30, 1871, Catasauqua, PA. Died: June 25, 1949, Wilkes-Barre, PA.
Height: 5'9"; weight: 150 lbs.; threw and batted left-handed.

Year	Club	League	Pos.	G	AB	R	H	2B	3B	HR	RBI	BA	PO	A	E	FA
1891	Washington	American Assn.	P	5	18	1	4	1	0	0	1	.222	0	10	3	.769
1898	Washington	National	OF	29	107	19	39	1	0	0	21	.364	39	5	1	.978
1899	Washington	National	OF-P	155	588	107	187	19	25	25*	122	.318	220	17	15	.940
1900	Boston	National	OF-1B	117	418	58	126	19	13	6	65	.301	278	16	12	.961
1901	Boston	American	OF-1B	129	490	86	169	23	15	12	114	.345	1279	55	36	.974
1902	Boston	American	OF	138	564	75	174	38	19	11	121*	.309	222	15	14	.944
1903	Boston	American	OF	141	567	74	163	39	20	13*	104*	.287	195	13	15	.933
1904	Boston	American	OF	157	597	64	167	20	19*	7	84	.280	216	14	11	.954
1905	Boston	American	OF-1B	130	455	59	109	20	8	3	59	.240	649	29	21	.970
1906	Boston	American	OF-1B	121	392	42	98	18	9	1	30	.250	472	50	9	.983
1907	Boston	American	OF	4	11	1	2	0	0	1	2	.182	6	0	0	1.000
Major League Totals: 11 years				1126	4207	586	1238	199	131	82	586	.294	3576	224	137	.965

WORLD SERIES RECORD

Year	Club	League	Pos.	G	AB	R	H	2B	3B	HR	RBI	BA	PO	A	E	FA
1903	Boston	American	OF	8	32	6	9	0	3	0	4	.281	8	0	0	1.000

*Indicates league leader

Michael (Gazook) Gazella

Born: October 13, 1891, Olyphant, PA. Died: September 11, 1978, Odessa, TX.
Height: 5'8"; weight: 165 lbs.; threw and batted right-handed.

Year	Club	League	Pos.	G	AB	R	H	2B	3B	HR	RBI	BA	PO	A	E	FA
1923	New York	American	SS-3B-2B	8	13	2	1	0	0	0	0	.077	4	9	0	1.000
1924	Minneapolis	American Assn.	3B-2B	151	512	92	139	29	11	12	—	.272	257	313	48	.917
1925	Atlanta	Southern Assn.	SS	137	465	80	142	27	13	7	65	.305	285	379	53	.926
1926	New York	American	3B-SS	66	168	21	39	6	0	0	21	.232	59	103	16	.910
1927	New York	American	3B-SS	54	115	17	32	8	4	0	9	.278	41	61	5	.953
1928	New York	American	3B-2B-SS	32	56	11	13	0	0	0	2	.232	10	31	3	.932
1929		VOLUNTARILY RETIRED														
1930	Hollywood	Pacific Coast	3B	171	650	103	197	44	2	11	94	.303	156	336	33	.937
1931	Hollywood	Pacific Coast	3B-SS	174	653	117	205	47	2	6	77	.314	142	372	42	.925
1932	Hollywood	Pacific Coast	3B	129	474	69	110	23	2	5	42	.232	101	277	25	.938
1934	Los Angeles	Pacific Coast	2B	83	235	47	62	7	1	7	47	.264	26	13	3	.929
1934	Ponca City	Western Assn.	2B	24	95	19	19	2	1	1	8	.200	48	57	8	.929
1935	Los Angeles	Pacific Coast	3B-2B-SS	51	116	16	22	4	1	1	13	.190	—	—	—	—
1935	Ponca City	Western Assn.	2B	28	61	10	20	4	0	0	6	.328	—	—	—	—

			Pos.	G	AB	R	H	2B	3B	HR	RBI	BA	PO	A	E	FA
Minor League Totals:	9 years		3B-2B-SS	948	3261	553	916	187	33	50	352	.281	—	—	—	—
Major League Totals:	4 years		3B-SS-2B	160	352	51	85	14	4	0	33	.241	114	204	24	.948

WORLD SERIES RECORD

Year	Club	League	Pos.	G	AB	R	H	2B	3B	HR	RBI	BA	PO	A	E	FA
1926	New York	American	3B	1	0	0	0	0	0	0	0	—	1	2	0	1.000

Peter Wyshner (Pete) Gray

Born: March 6, 1915, Nanticoke, PA.
Height: 6'1"; weight: 169 lbs.; threw and batted left-handed.

Year	Club	League	Pos.	G	AB	R	H	2B	3B	HR	RBI	BA	PO	A	E	FA
1942	Three Rivers	Canadien-American	OF	42	160	31	61	5	0	0	13	.381	111	1	1	.991
1943	Memphis	Southern Association	OF	126	453	56	131	7	6	0	42	.289	312	3	8	.975
1944	Memphis	Southern Association	OF	129	501	119	167	21	9	5	60	.333	336	5	6	.983
1945	St. Louis	American	OF	77	234	26	51	6	2	0	13	.218	162	3	7	.959
1946	Toledo	American Association	OF	48	96	14	24	3	0	0	7	.250	49	0	4	.925
1947		VOLUNTARILY RETIRED														
1948	Elmira	Eastern	OF	82	269	37	78	7	2	0	14	.290	120	2	6	.953
1949	Dallas	Texas	OF	45	56	18	12	2	0	0	5	.214	7	0	0	1.000
Minor League Totals:	6 years		OF	472	1595	282	490	45	17	6	149	.307	935	11	25	.971
Major League Totals:	1 year		OF	77	234	26	51	6	2	0	13	.218	162	3	7	.959

Stanley Raymond (Bucky) Harris

Born: November 8, 1896, at Port Jervis, NY. Died: November 8, 1977, at Bethesda, MD.

Height: 5'9"; weight: 156 lbs.; threw and batted right-handed. Manager, 1924–56: 2160 wins / 2218 losses. Named to Hall of Fame in 1975.

Year	Club	League	Pos.	G	AB	R	H	2B	3B	HR	RBI	BA	PO	A	E	FA
1916	Muskegon	Central	3B	55	169	8	28	—	—	—	—	.166	82	91	21	.892
1917	Norfolk	Virginia	SS	15	50	4	6	0	0	0	2	.120	40	34	14	.841
1917	Reading	New York	2B	75	280	44	70	—	—	—	—	.250	153	214	26	.934
1918	Buffalo	International	2B-SS	85	320	51	77	11	7	0	—	.241	216	273	34	.935
1919	Buffalo	International	2B	120	447	68	126	18	8	2	—	.282	281	366	41	.940
1919	Washington	American	2B	8	28	0	6	1	0	0	4	.214	21	27	4	.923
1920	Washington	American	2B	137	506	76	152	26	6	1	68	.300	345	401	33	.958
1921	Washington	American	2B	154	584	82	169	22	8	0	54	.289	407	481	38	.959
1922	Washington	American	2B	154	602	95	162	24	8	2	40	.269	479*	483	30	.970
1923	Washington	American	2B	145	532	60	150	21	13	2	70	.282	418*	449	35*	.961
1924	Washington	American	2B	143	544	88	146	28	9	1	58	.268	393	386	26	.968
1925	Washington	American	2B	144	551	91	158	30	3	1	66	.287	402	429	26	.970
1926	Washington	American	2B	141	537	94	152	39	9	1	63	.283	356*	427	30	.963
1927	Washington	American	2B	128	475	98	127	20	3	1	55	.267	316*	413	21	.972*
1928	Washington	American	2B	99	358	34	73	11	5	0	28	.204	251	326	18	.970
1929	Detroit	American	2B-SS	7	11	3	1	0	0	0	0	.091	5	13	2	.900
1930	Detroit	American		DID NOT PLAY												
1931	Detroit	American	2B	4	8	1	1	1	0	0	0	.125	5	6	0	1.000
Minor League Totals:	5 years			350	1266	175	307	29	15	2		.242	772	978	136	.928
Major League Totals:	12 years			1264	4736	722	1297	223	64	9	506	.274	3398	3841	263	.965

WORLD SERIES RECORD

Year	Club	League	Pos.	G	AB	R	H	2B	3B	HR	RBI	BA	PO	A	E	FA
1924	Washington	American	2B	7	33	5	11	0	0	2	7	.333	26	28	2	.694
1925	Washington	American	2B	7	23	2	2	0	0	0	0	.087	24	18	0	1.000
World Series Totals:	2 years		2B	14	56	7	13	0	0	2	7	.232	50	46	2	.980

*Indicates league leader

Hugh Ambrose (Hughie) Jennings

Born: April 2, 1870, at Pittston, PA. Died: February 1, 1928, at Scranton, PA.
Height: 5'8"; weight: 165 lbs.; threw and batted right-handed. Manager, 1907–20, 1924:
1131 wins / 932 losses. Named to Hall of Fame in 1945.

Year	Club	Pos.	League	G	AB	R	H	2B	3B	HR	RBI	BA	PO	A	E	FA
1890	Allentown	SS	Eastern Int.	13	50	8	16	—	—	.320	—	—	.934			
1891	Louisville	1B-SS	American Assn	81	316	46	95	10	8	1	58	.300	173	205	40	.904
1892	Louisville	SS	National	152	584	66	137	16	3	2	61	.232	336*	543	84	.912
1893	Louisville-Balt.	SS	National	38	135	12	25	3	0	2	15	.192	84	120	23	.898
1894	Baltimore	SS	National	128	505	136	168	27	20	4	109	.332	307*	497	62	.928*
1895	Baltimore	SS	National	131	528	159	204	40	8	4	125	.385	425*	460	53	.943*
1896	Baltimore	SS	National	129	523	125	208	24	9	0	121	.398	380*	476	68	.926
1897	Baltimore	SS	National	115	436	131	154	22	9	2	79	.353	336	417	54	.933*
1898	Baltimore	2B-SS	National	143	533	136	173	24	9	0	87	.325	361	435	60	.930
1899	Baltimore-Brkln	1B-2B-SS	National	63	223	44	67	5	10	0	42	.300	475	22	8	.984
1900	Brooklyn	1B	National	112	440	62	119	17	7	2	69	.270	1052	74	18	.984
1901	Philadelphia	1B	National	81	302	38	83	22	2	1	39	.274	725	39	15	.980
1902	Philadelphia	1B-2B-SS	National	78	289	31	80	16	3	1	32	.277	659	47	12	.983
1903	Brooklyn	OF	National	6	17	2	4	0	0	0	1	.235	7	0	0	1.000
1903	Baltimore	SS-2B	Eastern	32	122	26	40	8	0	0	4	.328	51	95	7	.954
1904	Baltimore	SS-2B	Eastern	92	332	65	97	21	0	1	0	.292	227	235	24	.951
1905	Baltimore	SS-2B	Eastern	56	179	24	45	8	0	0	2	.251	134	158	37	.887
1906	Baltimore	SS-2B	Eastern	75	242	24	60	9	1	0	0	.248	177	192	24	.928
1907	Detroit	SS	American	2	4	0	1	1	0	0	0	.250	0	2	0	1.000
1908	Detroit	PH	American	1	0	0	0	0	0	0	0	.000	0	0	0	.000
1909	Detroit	1B	American	2	4	1	2	0	0	0	0	.500	1	0	0	1.000
1912	Detroit	PH	American	1	1	0	0	0	0	0	0	.000	0	0	0	.000
1918	Detroit	1B	American	1	0	0	0	0	0	0	0	.000	0	0	0	.000
Minor League Totals: 5 years		SS-2B		268	925	147	258	46	1	1	6	.288	589	680	92	.931
Major League Totals: 18 years		SS-1B-2B		1264	4840	989	1520	227	88	19	838	.314	5321	3337	497	.946

*Indicates League Leader

Christopher (Christy) Mathewson

Born: August 12, 1880, at Factoryville, PA. Died: October 7, 1925, at Saranac Lake, NY. Height: 6'1"; weight: 195 lbs.; threw and batted right-handed. Manager, 1916–18: 164 wins / 176 losses. Named to Hall of Fame in 1936.

Year	Club	League	G	IP	W	L	Pct.	H	R	ER	SO	BB	ERA
1899	Taunton	New England	17	—	5	2	.714	—	—	—	—	—	—
1900	Norfolk	Virginia	22	187	20	2	.909	119	59	—	128	27	—
1900	New York	National	6	34	0	3	.000	34	32	—	15	20	—
1901	New York	National	40	336	20	17	.541	281	131	—	215	92	—
1902	New York	National	34	276	14	17	.452	241	114	—	162	74	—
1903	New York	National	45	367	30	13	.698	321	136	—	267*	100	—
1904	New York	National	48	368	33	12	.733	306	120	—	212*	78	—
1905	New York	National	43	339	31*	9	.775	252	85	—	206*	64	—
1906	New York	National	38	267	22	12	.647	262	100	—	128	77	—
1907	New York	National	41	315	24*	12	.667	250	88	—	178*	53	—
1908	New York	National	56*	391*	37*	11	.771	281	85	—	259*	42	—
1909	New York	National	37	274	25	6	.806	192	57	—	149	36	—
1910	New York	National	38	319	27*	9	.750	291	98	—	190*	57	—
1911	New York	National	45	307	26	13	.667	303*	102	—	141	38	2.12
1912	New York	National	43	310+	23	12	.657	311	107	73	134	34	2.06*
1913	New York	National	40	306	25	11	.694	291+	93	70	93	21	3.00
1914	New York	National	41	312	24	13	.648	314	133	104*	80	23	3.58
1915	New York	National	27	186	8	14	.364	199	97	74	57	20	3.58
1916	New York–Cin	National	13	74	4	4	.500	74	35	25	19	8	3.04

			G	IP	W	L	Pct.	H	R	ER	SO	BB	ERA
Minor League Totals:	2 years		39	—	25	4	.812	—	—	—	—	—	—
Major League Totals:	17 years		635	4781	373	188	.665	4203	1613	—	2505	837	—

WORLD SERIES RECORD

Year	Club	League	G	IP	W	L	Pct.	H	R	ER	SO	BB	ERA
1905	New York	National	3	27	3	0	.000	14	0	0	18	1	0.00
1911	New York	National	3	27	1	2	.333	25	8	6	13	2	2.00
1912	New York	National	3	28	0	2	.000	23	11	5	10	5	1.57
1913	New York	National	2	19	1	1	.500	14	3	2	7	2	0.95

			G	IP	W	L	Pct.	H	R	ER	SO	BB	ERA
World Series Totals:	4 years		11	101	5	5	.500	76	22	13	48	10	1.15

*Indicates league leader. +Indicates tied for league lead

John Edward (Honest Eddie) Murphy

Born: October 2, 1891, at Hancock, NY. Died: February 21, 1969, at Dunmore, PA.
Height: 5'9"; weight: 155 lbs.; threw right-handed; batted left-handed.

Year	Club	League	Pos.	G	AB	R	H	2B	3B	HR	RBI	BA	PO	A	E	FA
1911	Scranton	New York State	OF-SS-2B	91	323	64	97	—	15	7	—	.300	176	33	12	.946
1912	Baltimore	International	OF	122	510	108	184	14	1	0	6	.361	174	15	17	.917
1912	Philadelphia	American	OF	33	142	24	45	4	7	1	6	.317	48	6	3	.947
1913	Philadelphia	American	OF	136	508	105	150	14	7	1	30	.295	166	14	11	.942
1914	Philadelphia	American	OF	148	573	101	156	12	9	3	43	.272	194	15	13	.941
1915	Phila.-Chicago	American	OF-3B	138	533	88	146	14	9	0	43	.274	177	30	16	.928
1916	Chicago	American	OF-3B	51	105	14	22	5	1	0	4	.210	28	2	1	.968
1917	Chicago	American	OF	53	51	9	16	2	1	0	16	.314	2	0	0	1.000
1918	Chicago	American	OF-2B	91	286	36	85	9	3	0	23	.297	124	18	7	.953
1919	Chicago	American	OF	30	35	8	17	4	0	0	5	.486	10	1	1	.917
1920	Chicago	American	OF-3B	58	118	22	40	2	1	0	19	.339	27	13	5	.889
1921	Chicago	American	OF	6	5	1	1	0	0	0	0	.200	0	0	0	—
1921	Columbus	American Assn.	OF	117	—	—	—	—	—	—	—	.293	—	—	—	—
1922	Columbus	American Assn.	OF	140	—	—	—	—	—	—	—	.317	—	—	—	—
1923	Columbus	American Assn.	OF	154	—	—	—	—	—	—	—	.351	—	—	—	—
1924	Columbus	American Assn.	OF	146	—	—	—	—	—	—	—	—	—	—	—	—
1925	Columbus	American Assn.	OF	100	390	82	155	21	5	3	71	.397	159	9	2	.988
1926	Pittsburgh	National	OF	16	17	3	2	0	0	0	6	.118	5	0	0	1.000
1927	Rochester	International	OF	83	305	56	104	27	4	1	52	.341	131	10	5	.966
1928	Montreal	International	OF	114	322	50	98	9	2	2	42	.304	135	11	3	.980
Minor League Totals:	9 years		OF-SS	1067	—							—				
Major League Totals:	11 years		OF-3B-2B	760	2373	411	680	66	32	4	195	.287	781	99	57	.939

WORLD SERIES RECORD

Year	Club	League	Pos.	G	AB	R	H	2B	3B	HR	RBI	BA	PO	A	E	FA
1913	Philadelphia	American	OF	5	22	2	5	0	0	0	0	.227	15	0	0	1.000
1914	Philadelphia	American	OF	4	16	2	3	2	0	0	0	.188	4	0	0	1.000
1919	Chicago	American	—	3	2	0	0	0	0	0	0	.000	—	—	—	—
World Series Totals:	3 years		OF	12	40	4	8	2	0	0	0	.200	19	0	0	1.000

Stephen Francis (Steve) O'Neill

Born: July 6, 1891, at Minooka, PA. Died: January 26, 1962, at Cleveland, OH.
Height: 5'10", weight: 165 lbs.; threw and batted right-handed. Manager, 1935–37, 1943–48, 1950–54: 1039 wins / 819 losses.

Year	Club	League	Pos.	G	AB	R	H	2B	3B	HR	RBI	BA	PO	A	E	FA
1910	Elmira	New York	C	28	95	5	19	2	0	0	—	.200	166	46	5	.977
1911	Worcester	New England	C	101	316	43	89	18	5	0	—	.282	444	113	15	.971
1911	Cleveland	American	C	9	27	1	4	1	0	0	1	.148	55	17	1	.986
1912	Cleveland	American	C	68	215	17	49	4	0	0	14	.228	316	108	17	.961
1913	Cleveland	American	C	78	234	19	69	13	3	0	29	.295	353	119	13	.973
1914	Cleveland	American	C-1B	86	269	28	68	12	2	0	20	.253	394	134	24	.957
1915	Cleveland	American	C	121	386	32	91	14	2	2	34	.236	556	175	24	.968
1916	Cleveland	American	C	130	378	30	89	23	0	0	29	.235	540	154	21	.971
1917	Cleveland	American	C	129	370	21	68	10	0	0	29	.184	446	145	12	.980
1918	Cleveland	American	C	114	359	34	87	8	2	1	35	.242	409	154	10	.983
1919	Cleveland	American	C	125	398	46	115	35	7	2	47	.289	472	125	14	.977
1920	Cleveland	American	C	149	489	63	157	39	5	3	55	.321	576	128	17	.976
1921	Cleveland	American	C	106	335	39	108	22	1	1	50	.322	393	92	9	.982
1922	Cleveland	American	C	133	392	33	122	27	4	2	65	.311	450	116	15	.974
1923	Cleveland	American	C	113	330	31	82	12	0	0	50	.248	354	68	14	.968
1924	Boston	American	C	106	307	29	73	15	1	0	38	.238	342	75	13	.970
1925	New York	American	C	35	91	7	26	5	0	1	13	.286	113	27	8	.946
1925	Reading	International	C	34	94	9	25	5	0	1	14	.266	85	22	4	.964
1926	Toronto	International	C	135	435	62	115	29	2	3	69	.264	631	84	10	.986
1927	St. Louis	American	C	74	191	14	44	7	0	1	22	.230	180	57	4	.983
1928	St. Louis	American	C	10	24	4	7	1	0	0	6	.292	19	4	1	.958
1929	Toronto	International	C	93	262	31	84	17	1	3	31	.321	338	60	7	.982
1930	Toronto	International	C	75	195	26	60	10	0	0	32	.308	269	45	5	.984
1931	Toronto	International	C	89	226	21	51	10	0	0	25	.226	310	46	6	.983
1932	Toledo	American Assn.	C	44	131	13	34	7	2	3	16	.260	288	39	8	.966
1933	Toledo	American Assn.	C	18	53	4	16	0	1	1	—	.302	78	17	1	.990
1934	Toledo	American Assn.	C	30	67	9	21	5	0	0	16	.313	64	10	4	.949
1942	Beaumont	Texas	C	1	3	0	1	0	0	0	0	.333	3	1	0	1.000

			Pos.	G	AB	R	H	2B	3B	HR	RBI	BA	PO	A	E	FA
Minor League Totals:	10 years		C	648	1877	223	515	103	11	11	—	.279	2676	483	65	.977
Major League Totals:	17 years		C-1B	1586	4795	448	1259	248	34	13	537	.263	5968	1698	217	.972

WORLD SERIES RECORD

Year	Club	League	Pos.	G	AB	R	H	2B	3B	HR	RBI	BA	PO	A	E	FA
1920	Cleveland	American	C	7	21	1	7	3	0	0	2	.333	23	6	1	.967

Joseph Paul ("Professor") Ostrowski

Born: November 15, 1916, at West Wyoming, PA.
Height: 6'0"; weight: 180 lbs.; threw and batted left-handed.

Year	Club	League	G	IP	W	L	Pct.	H	R	ER	SO	BB	ERA
1941	Centerville	Eastern Shore	17	126	10	4	.714	91	34	24	74	29	1.71
1941	Canton	Mid-Atlantic	6	40	2	3	.400	52	28	21	11	25	4.73
1942	Greensboro	Piedmont	35	156	21	8	.724	209	69	47	120	49	1.65
1943–45		IN MILITARY SERVICE											
1946	Louisville	American Association	24	116	10	4	.714	123	48	37	54	35	2.87
1947	Louisville	American Association	29	184	13	11	.542	160	75	61	66	43	2.98
1948	Toledo	American Association	19	115	6	9	.400	129	65	58	51	22	4.54
1948	St. Louis	American	26	78	4	6	.400	108	54	52	20	17	6.00
1949	St. Louis	American	40	141	8	8	.500	185	94	75	34	27	4.79
1950	St. Louis-NY	American	30	101	3	5	.375	107	48	41	30	22	3.65
1951	New York	American	34	95	6	4	.600	103	44	37	30	18	3.51
1952	New York	American	20	40	2	2	.500	56	35	29	17	14	5.63
Minor League Totals: 6 years			130	737	62	39	.582	764	319	248	376	203	3.08
Major League Totals: 5 years			150	455	23	25	.479	559	275	234	131	98	4.54

WORLD SERIES RECORD

Year	Club	League	G	IP	W	L	Pct.	H	R	ER	SO	BB	ERA
1951	New York	American	1	2	0	0	.000	1	1	0	1	0	0.00

Stanley Walter (Stan) Pawloski

Born: September 6, 1931, at Wanamie, PA.
Height: 6'1"; weight: 175 lbs.; threw and batted right-handed.

Year	Club	League	Pos.	G	AB	R	H	2B	3B	HR	RBI	BA	PO	A	E	FA
1949	Stroudsburg	North Atlantic	3B	87	307	46	101	17	7	4	64	.329	89	213	21	.935
1950	Pittsfield	Canadian-Amer.	3B	125	429	59	116	23	3	3	59	.270	135	237	27	.932
1951	Cedar Rapids	Three-I	2B-3B	118	427	66	119	24	4	9	75	.279	297	310	34	.929
1952	Reading	Eastern	2B	134	465	70	126	25	6	7	63	.272	324	345	13	.981
1953		IN MILITARY SERVICE														
1954	Indianapolis	American Assn.	2B-3B	55	164	14	46	11	0	1	12	.280	89	94	4	.979
1955	Indianapolis	American Assn.	2B-3B	140	490	72	131	23	7	14	80	.267	282	330	23	.946
1955	Cleveland	American	—	2	8	0	1	0	0	0	0	.125	—	—	—	—
1956	Indianapolis	American Assn.	3B-2B	124	397	56	96	19	2	10	53	.242	155	269	15	.973
1957	San Diego	Pacific Coast	2B-3B	18	31	4	6	1	0	0	3	.194	—	—	—	—
1958	Mobile	Southern Assn.	2B	143	484	57	115	20	1	7	36	.238	324	441	19	.976
Minor League Totals:	9 years		3B-2B	944	3194	444	856	163	30	55	445	.263	—	—	—	—
Major League Totals:	1 year			2	8	0	1	0	0	0	0	.125	—	—	—	—

John Picus (Jack) Quinn

Born: July 5, 1884, at Mahanoy City, PA. Died: April 17, 1946, at Pottsville, PA.
Height: 6'0"; weight: 200 lbs.; threw and batted right-handed.

Year	Club	League	G	IP	W	L	Pct.	H	R	ER	SO	BB	ERA
1907	Macon	South Atlantic	15	109	6	5	.545	83	—	—	60	33	—
1908	Richmond	Virginia	17	—	14	0	1.000	102	—	—	92	20	—
1909	New York	American	22	118	9	5	.643	110	45	—	35	24	—
1910	New York	American	35	237	18	12	.600	214	88	—	82	58	—
1911	New York	American	39	175	8	9	.471	203	111	—	71	41	—
1912	New York	American	18	103	5	7	.417	139	89	—	47	23	—
1912	Rochester	International	13	108	8	4	.667	94	39	—	44	14	—
1913	Rochester	International	38	268	19	13	.594	261	111	—	153	62	—
1913	Boston	National	8	56	4	3	.571	55	22	15	33	7	2.41
1914	Baltimore	Federal	46	339	26	14	.650	330*	121	101	165	63	2.68
1915	Baltimore	Federal	44	275	9	22*	.290	291	139	102	116	64	3.34
1916	Vernon	Pacific Coast	51	289	16	13	.552	292	125	94	149	85	2.93
1917	Vernon	Pacific Coast	52	409	24	20	.545	415	155	107	160	84	2.35
1918	Vernon	Pacific Coast	24	—	12	6	.667	—	—	—	—	—	—
1918	Chicago	American	6	51	5	1	.833	38	13	13	22	7	2.29
1919	New York	American	38	264	15	15	.500	242	96	77	97	65	2.63
1920	New York	American	41	253	18	10	.643	271	110	90	101	48	3.20
1921	New York	American	33	129	8	7	.533	158	61	50	44	32	3.49

(Jack Quinn continued)

Year	Club	League	G	IP	W	L	Pct.	H	R	ER	SO	BB	ERA
1922	Boston	American	40	256	13	15	.464	263	119	99	67	59	3.48
1923	Boston	American	42	243	13	17	.433	302	125	105	71	53	3.89
1924	Boston	American	43	228	12	13	.480	237	107	81	64	51	3.20
1925	Boston-Phila.	American	37	205	13	11	.542	259	124	94	43	42	4.13
1926	Philadelphia	American	31	164	10	11	.476	191	74	62	58	36	3.40
1927	Philadelphia	American	34	207	15	10	.600	211	82	73	43	37	3.17
1928	Philadelphia	American	31	211	18	7	.720	239	92	68	43	34	2.90
1929	Philadelphia	American	35	161	11	9	.550	182	87	71	41	39	3.97
1930	Philadelphia	American	35	90	9	7	.563	109	51	44	28	22	4.40
1931	Brooklyn	National	39	64	5	4	.556	65	28	19	25	24	2.67
1932	Brooklyn	National	42	87	3	7	.300	102	36	32	28	24	3.31
1933	Cincinnati	National	14	16	0	1	.000	20	9	7	3	5	3.94
1934	Hollywood	Pacific Coast	6	18	1	1	.500	29	12	12	3	4	6.00
1935	Johnstown	Mid-Atlantic	1	2	0	0	.000	2	0	0	0	0	0.00
Minor League Totals:	9 years		217	—	100	62		—	—	—	—	—	—
Major League Totals:	21 years		663	3318	212	181	.539	3610	1569	—	1046	731	—
World Series Totals:	3 years (1921, '29, '30)		3	10.2	0	1	.000	18	11	10	5	4	8.44

*Indicates league leader

Joseph Benjamin (Lefty) Shaute

Born: August 1, 1899, at Peckville, PA. Died: February 21, 1970, at Scranton, PA.
Height: 6'0"; weight: 190 lbs.; threw and batted left-handed.

Year	Club	League	G	IP	W	L	Pct.	H	SO	BB	ERA
1922	Cleveland	American	2	3	0	0	.000	7	3	3	19.64
1923	Cleveland	American	33	172	10	8	.556	176	61	53	3.51
1924	Cleveland	American	46	283	20	17*	.541	317	68	83	3.75
1925	Cleveland	American	26	131	4	12	.250	160	34	44	5.43
1926	Cleveland	American	34	206	14	10	.583	215	47	65	3.53
1927	Cleveland	American	45	230	9	16	.360	255	63	75	4.22
1928	Cleveland	American	36	253	13	17	.433	295	81	68	4.04
1929	Cleveland	American	26	162	8	8	.500	211	43	52	4.28
1930	Toronto	International	6	—	3	1	—	—	—	—	—
1930	Cleveland	American	4	4	0	0	—	8	2	4	15.43
1931	Brooklyn	National	25	128	11	8	.579	162	50	32	4.83
1932	Brooklyn	National	34	117	7	7	.500	147	32	21	4.62
1933	Brooklyn	National	41	108	3	4	.429	125	26	31	3.49
1934	Cincinnati	National	8	17	0	2	.000	19	2	3	4.15
1934	Scranton	New York–Penna.	28	187	16	3	.842	221	95	29	3.80
1934	Minneapolis	American Assn.	2	10	1	0	1.000	—	—	—	—
1935	Scranton	New York–Penna.	31	206	21	7	.750	218	87	38	2.84
1936	Scranton	New York–Penna.	32	239	20	7	.741	283	98	34	4.03
1937	Scranton	New York–Penna.	23	142	9	9	.500	165	59	25	3.81
1938	Wilkes–Barre	Eastern	23	136	6	11	.353	151	59	20	3.83

			G	IP	W	L	Pct.	H	SO	BB	ERA
Minor League Totals: 7 years			145	—	76	38	—	—	—	—	—
Major League Totals: 13 years			360	1816	99	109	—	2097	512	534	4.15

Edward Augustine (Ed) Walsh

Born: May 14, 1881, at Plains, PA. Died: May 26, 1959, at Pompano Beach, FLA.
Height: 6'1"; weight: 193 lbs.; threw and batted right-handed. Named to Hall of Fame in 1946.

Year	Club	League	G	IP	W	L	Pct.	H	R	SO	BB	ERA
1902	Wilkes-Barre	Pennsylvania State	4	36	1	2	.333	31	—	20	8	—
1902	Meriden	Connecticut	21	182	15	5	.750	125	—	98	48	—
1903	Meriden	Connecticut	23	182	11	10	.524	135	—	126	46	—
1903	Newark	Eastern	19	117	9	5	.643	70	—	77	28	—
1904	Chicago	American	18	113	6	3	.667	83	37	52	34	2.60
1905	Chicago	American	22	138	8	3	.727	128	56	71	35	2.17
1906	Chicago	American	42	281	17	13	.567	214	90	171	58	1.88
1907	Chicago	American	56*	419*	24	18	.600	330	123	207	85	1.60*
1908	Chicago	American	66*	465*	40*	15	.727*	343*	111	269*	56	1.42
1909	Chicago	American	31	230	15	11	.577	166	52	127	50	1.41
1910	Chicago	American	45+	370	18	20*	.474	242	90	258	61	1.27*
1911	Chicago	American	56*	369*	27	18	.600	327	125	255*	72	2.22
1912	Chicago	American	62*	393*	27	17	.614	332*	125	254	94	2.15
1913	Chicago	American	16	98	8	3	.727	91	37	34	39	2.58
1914	Chicago	American	9	45	2	3	.400	33	19	14	20	2.82
1915	Chicago	American	3	27	3	0	1.000	18	4	12	6	1.33
1916	Chicago	American	2	3	0	1	.000	6	3	3	1	2.70
1917	Boston	National	4	18	0	1	.000	22	9	4	9	3.50
1919	Milwaukee	American Assn.	4	21	2	2	.500	22	—	6	8	—
1920	Bridgeport	Eastern	3	22	1	1	.500	22	—	6	6	—
Minor League Totals: 6 years			74	560	39	25	.542	405	—	333	144	—
Major League Totals: 14 years			432	2969	195	126	.607	2235	881	1731	620	1.82

WORLD SERIES RECORD

Year	Club	League	G	IP	W	L	Pct.	H	R	SO	BB	ERA
1906	Chicago	American	2	15	2	0	1.000	7	6	17	6	1.80

*Indicates league leader. +Indicates tied for league lead

Notes

1. Growing Up in Coal Country

1. Donald L. Miller & Richard E. Sharpless, *The Kingdom of Coal: Work, Enterprise and Ethnic Communities in the Mine Fields* (Philadelphia: University of Pennsylvania, 1985), 3–5.

2. *Ibid.*, 52–68.

3. Commonwealth of Pennsylvania, *Report of the Department of the Mines of Pennsylvania, Part I — Anthracite* (Harrisburg, PA: Commonwealth of Pennsylvania, 1924), 18.

4. Oscar Handlin in his Pulitzer Prize winning work, *The Uprooted: The Epic Story of the Great Migrations That Made the American People* (New York: Grosset & Dunlap, 1951), was the first historian to concentrate on Eastern European assimilation into American life. He emphasized the importance of ethnic consciousness as an important first step in the assimilation process, particularly in urban areas where the members of the same ethnic group would congregate in order to translate their new American culture. A decade later, John Higham offered a more compelling argument by attributing nativism as the primary motivating force in forcing immigrants to assimilate. Nativist attitudes demanded that immigrants conform to traditional Protestant-American values. See Higham, *Strangers in the Land: Patterns of American Nativism, 1860–1925* (New York: Atheneum, 1967).

Michael Barendse, *Social Expectations & Perception: The Case of the Slavic Anthracite Workers* (State College, PA: Pennsylvania State University, 1981) and Victor Greene, *For God and Country: The Rise of Polish and Lithuanian Ethnic Consciousness in America, 1860–1910* (Madison, WI: Historical Society of Wisconsin,

1975) both agree with Higham's argument and apply it to the Polish and Lithuanian immigrants of northeastern Pennsylvania. They add that for these two ethnic groups, the assimilation process was interrupted by a split labor market divided along ethnic lines. This split market resulted in severe social animosities between the newly arrived Eastern Europeans and the members of the more established Northern European immigrants, most notably the English and Welsh.

5. Miller & Sharpless, *Kingdom of Coal*, 242, 259.

6. Harold Aurand, "Child Labor and the Welfare of Children in an Anthracite Coal Mining Town," *Coal Towns: A Contemporary Perspective, 1899–1923*, ed. Harold Aurand (Lexington, MA: Ginn Custom Publishing, 1980), 54; and Peter Roberts, *Anthracite Coal Communities* (New York, 1904), 181.

7. Susan Campbell Bartoletti, *Growing Up in Coal Country* (Boston: Houghton Mifflin Company, 1996), 14–15.

8. Stan Coveleski quoted in Lawrence S. Ritter, *The Glory of Their Times: The Story of the Early Days of Baseball Told by the Men Who Played It* (reprint, New York: Vintage Books, 1985), 118.

9. Coveleski quoted in "Talkers Don't Gain a Thing — Coveleski," *Wilkes-Barre Record*: January 6, 1947. See also Mark Gilger, "Stan Coveleski's World Series record remains intact," *The News-Item* (Shamokin, PA): October 21–22, 2000. Of the four older Coveleskie brothers, Jake was considered to be the best pitcher. His professional career, which began with the Shamokin club of the Atlantic League, was cut short by the Spanish-American War. He was killed in the Philippines. Frank was also a pitcher for Shamokin, but made his way to the International and Federal Leagues before his pro career ended. John was a third baseman and outfielder for Shamokin, Lancaster and Erie before cracking the majors as a utility infielder for the Philadelphia Athletics and, later, the St. Louis Browns. Encouraged by John, Stanley made his own bid to become a major leaguer. Aside from Stanley, Harry Coveleskie was the most successful of the five brothers. He pitched in the majors for nine seasons with the Philadelphia Phillies, Cincinnati Reds and Detroit Tigers. Although he enjoyed three outstanding seasons with Detroit, winning 66 games and losing 35 during that span, Harry is best remembered as the Phillies' "Giant Killer," who, in 1908, defeated the New York Giants in three games over the brief span of five days to knock them out of the pennant race. Stanley not only distinguished himself from his brothers with his Hall of Fame career, but also by dropping the letter "e" from his last name.

10. Coveleski in Ritter, *Glory of Their Times*, 118–119.

11. Joe Boley quoted in Bartoletti, *Growing Up in Coal Country*, 87.

12. Reverend John Whitney Evans in his essay, "Jack Quinn: Stitching a Baseball Legend" (unpublished manuscript, 1997), 1–4, notes that Quinn purposely kept the sportswriters guessing about the year of his birth, giving, at various times 1883, '84 or '85. Just as elusive was his place of birth. Alleged birthplaces include Hazleton, Mahanoy City and Stockton as well as Jeanesville, all of which are located in Pennsylvania's anthracite region.

13. John Picus Quinn quoted in Will Wedge, "The Story of John P. Quinn," *The New York Sun*: June 21, 1929.

14. Gordon Mackay, "Jack Quinn Hurled Ball Up the Hill," *The Philadelphia Inquirer*: August 2, 1925.

15. John Picus Quinn quoted in Bill Dooly, "Baseball's Oldest Major League Hurler Leads Athletics Sharpshooters," *The Philadelphia Record*: July 22, 1928.

16. Quinn quoted in Austen Lake, "Saga of Homeless One Who Became 'Old Jack' Quinn," *New York Daily Transcript*, n.d. (circa 1932), Jack Quinn File, National Baseball Library.

17. Quinn quoted in F. C. Lane, "The Dream of Major League Pitchers," *Baseball Magazine*, March 1927, 453.

18. Ed Walsh quoted in Frank Monardo, "Pitching Only 30 percent Now — Walsh," *The Sporting News*, January 9, 1957.

19. Bartoletti, *Growing Up in Coal Country*, 34–37.

20. Hugh Fullerton, "At-a-Boy! How Hughey Jennings Fought His Way from the Mine Pits to the Pinnacle of Baseball Glory," *Liberty Magazine*, April 14, 1928, 49–50.

21. John Brown, "Hugh Jennings: The Live Wire of Modern Baseball," *Baseball Magazine*, April 1910, 36.

22. John H. Gruber, "Coal Digger When a Youth, Now He's a Batting Champion," *Philadelphia Public Ledger*, March 7, 1915.

23. "O'Neill Quit Mines to Start Baseball Career," *Cleveland Plain Dealer*, August 5, 1935.

24. Steve O'Neill quoted in Cy Kritzer, "O'Neill Always a 'Ball Players' Pilot'," *The Sporting News*, July 5, 1950.

25. Brown, "Hugh Jennings," 36.

26. Pete Wyshner Gray interview, Nanticoke, PA, June 26, 1989.

27. Pete Wyshner Gray interview, Nanticoke, PA, August 8, 1989.

28. Ray Robinson, *Matty: An American Hero* (New York: Oxford University Press, 1993), 9–11.

29. Mrs. William B. Meloney, "The Mother of Christy Mathewson Wanted Her Son to Be a Preacher," *The Delineator*, August 8, 1912.

30. Joe Byron, "The Class Picture, 1893" from the Bucknell University Archives.

31. Christy Mathewson, "How to Pitch, Part I: How I Gained Control and How You May Do It," *American Boy*, May 1916, 4.

32. Ray Snyder quoted in Bill Keisling, "Mathewson's Catcher of Early Days Is Marking 79th Birthday," *The Scrantonian*, May 29, 1960.

33. Robinson, *Matty*, 15–16.

34. Mathewson, "How to Pitch, Part I," 4.

35. Joseph G. Butash, "Diogenes Your Search Is Over!" *Scranton/Wilkes-Barre Red Barons 1991 Yearbook*, 9.

36. For the most recent and comprehensive treatment of the Molly Maguires see Kevin Kenny, *Making Sense of the Molly Maguires* (New York: Oxford University Press, 1998). Kenny offers a much needed corrective to the traditional historiography of the Molly Maguires which depicts the group as Irish terrorists who were justifiably crushed by the Pinkerton Detective Agency. Instead, Kenny provides a more sympathetic treatment that focuses on the larger conflict between the mine owners and their workers. He argues that the Mollies were angered by their miserable working conditions, alienated by the clergy and hierarchy of the Catholic Church to which they belonged, frustrated by the owners' ability to prevent union activity, and angered by their political influence that denied any legal recourse.

While Kenny does not deny the violent nature of the Mollies' actions, he does identify the inconsistencies of Pinkerton detective James McParlan's testimony — which condemned the Mollies to the hangman's noose.

37. Barendse, *Social Expectations*, 15–17.

38. Ibid., 53–56.

39. Craig Phelan, *Divided Loyalties: The Public and Private Life of Labor Leader John Mitchell* (New York: State University of New York Press, 1994), 123–190.

40. *Pennsylvania Mine Reports* (1901), 12. Of the total work force of 59,823 men who worked in the collieries of the Northern coalfield, 36,381 were of eastern or southern European origin. And 40 percent of these were, more specifically, Lithuanian or Polish.

41. Pete Wyshner Gray interview: February 6, 1990.

42. See *Wilkes-Barre Times Leader*: May 7, 9; and June 3, 7, 1935.

43. Pete Wyshner Gray interview, February 6, 1990.

44. Joseph Ostrowski interview, West Wyoming, PA, January 10, 2000.

45. Stan Pawloski interview, Philadelphia, PA, June 16, 1999.

2. Anthracite Leagues

1. Pete Gray interview: October 15, 1993.

2. Mathewson, "How I Came to Be a Big League Pitcher" and Robinson, *Matty*, 13.

3. "If You Can't Boost, Don't Knock," *Philadelphia Inquirer*: October 17, 1932.

4. Jack Picus Quinn quoted in "Jack Quinn," American League News Service Bureau Release, Chicago, Illinois: February 24, 1929; see also Lee Allen, "Baseball Methuselah — Jack Quinn, Big Leaguer at 49," *The Sporting News*: September 9, 1962.

5. Hugh Fullerton, "At-a-Boy! How Hughey Jennings Fought His Way from the Mine Pits to the Pinnacle of Baseball Glory," *Liberty Magazine* (April 14, 1928): 50; and John Brown, "Hugh Jennings: The Live Wire of Modern Baseball," *Baseball Magazine* (July 1910): 37.

6. John C. Chapman, "How I Discovered Hughie Jennings," *Baseball Magazine* (July 1910), 25; and J. C. Koford, "Breaking into the Baseball Game," *Sporting Life*: March 25, 1916.

7. Martin Corcoran to Sid C. Keener, Director, National Baseball Hall of Fame, November 22, 1957. National Baseball Library.

8. Ed Walsh, "Pitching Only 30 Percent Now — Walsh," *The Sporting News*: January 9, 1957.

9. Stanley Coveleskie interview, Cooperstown, NY: July 1969. National Baseball Library.

10. Joseph G. Butash, "Diogenes, Your Search Is Over!" 1991 Scranton / *Wilkes-Barre Red Barons Yearbook*, 9.

11. *Wilkes-Barre Times Leader*: June 25, 1949; Van Rose, "When a Home Run Champ Was the Hometown Hero," *Wilkes-Barre Times Leader*: September 21, 1998; and Charles A. McCarthy, "Wilkes-Barre Homer King, 'Bucky' Freeman, Set Big League Mark in 1899," *Wilkes-Barre Sunday Independent*: April 18, 1976.

12. Robinson, *Matty*, 16.

13. Mathewson, "Mathewson, Starting Thirteenth Season with Giants, Tells of Early Trials That Beset His Advent in Baseball," *New York Evening Telegram*: April 2, 1912.

14. Robinson, *Matty*, 17–18.

15. "Bucky Has Climbed to Dizzy Heights from Deep in Coal Mines," *Washington Evening Star*: September 19, 1924.

16. Coveleski, *Glory of Their Times*, 117–18.

17. Cy Kritzer, "O'Neill Always a 'Ball Player's Pilot'," *The Sporting News*: July 5, 1950.

18. Chic Feldmen, "Indians Paid Shaute $6,000 for Winning 20 Games in 1924," *The Scrantonian*: December 25, 1966.

19. Mickey O'Neill quoted in *Toronto Star Weekly*: March 24, 1945.

20. *St. Louis Post-Dispatch*: December 12, 1944: and *Memphis Press-Scimitar*: September 29, 1944.

21. See "If You Can't Boost, Don't Knock," *Philadelphia Inquirer*: October 17, 1932; Gray Interview: August 8, 1989; and "John Picus (Jack) Quinn," *Wilkes-Barre Record*: December 22, 1933.

22. *Wilkes-Barre Times Leader*: July 10, 1933.

23. Pawloski interview.

24. Harry Dorish interview, Kingston, PA: December 30, 1999.

25. Jerry Izenberg, "Bilko Never Saw the Promised Land," *New York Post*: March 9, 1978.

26. Bob Duliba interview, West Pittston, PA: May 23, 1999.

27. Ostrowski interview.

28. Bob Krawczeniuk, "Nestor Chylak Jr. to Become Eighth Umpire in Hall of Fame," *Scranton Sunday Times*: July 25, 1999.

29. Chic Feldman, "Paparella American League Senior Umpire," *Scrantonian*: January 20, 1963.

30. James Isaminger, "If You Can't Boost, Don't Knock," *Philadelphia Inquirer*: October 17, 1926.

3. Chasing the Dream

1. Neil J. Sullivan, *The Minors: The Struggles and the Triumph of Baseball's Poor Relation from 1876 to the Present* (New York: St. Martin's Press, 1990), viii, 1–42.

2. Tom Mooney, "Pro Baseball Hit Wilkes-Barre More Than a Century Ago," *Times Leader*: December 19, 1999.

3. Nicholas E. Petula, *A History of Scranton Professional Baseball, 1865–1953* (Scranton, PA: 1989), 9; and Mike Cummings, "History of the Scranton/Wilkes-Barre Franchise," *Red Barons Baseball 1999 Yearbook*, 5.

4. Mooney, "Pro Baseball Hit Wilkes-Barre."

5. Cummings, "History of Scranton/Wilkes-Barre," 6; and Lloyd Wagner, "History of the AAA Alliance," *Scranton/Wilkes-Barre Red Barons 1989 Scorecard Magazine*, 58.

6. Cummings, "History of Scranton/Wilkes-Barre," 6.

7. Petula, *A History of Scranton Professional Baseball, 1865–1953*, 12–19.

During the period 1905 to 1915, the Scranton Miners were owned, at various times by John Barnes, proprietor of the Brunswick Hotel; Edward Coleman, a Scranton businessman; and Robert W. Allen, president of the Anthracite Brewing Company.

8. Ed Walsh as told to Frank Monardo, "Pitching Only 30 Percent Now — Walsh," *The Sporting News*: January 9, 1957.

9. Ibid.

10. Charles A. McCarthy, "Wilkes-Barre Homer King, 'Bucky' Freeman, Set Big League Mark in 1899," *Sunday Independent*: April 18, 1976.

11. Stan Coveleski quoted in Ritter, *Glory of Their Times*, 121.

12. Coveleski interview, National Baseball Library: July 1969.

13. Ford Sawyer, "First Sacker Still a Star," *Boston Globe*: August 5, 1924.

14. George Stovall quoted in "Coal Miner to Champion — Is Daubert's Life Story," *Baseball Magazine* June 1914): 12.

15. John H. Gruber, "Coal Digger When a Youth, Now He's a Batting Champion," *Philadelphia Public Ledger*: March 7, 1915.

16. "Bucky Has Climbed to Dizzy Heights from Deep in Coal Mines," *Washington Evening Star*: September 19, 1924.

17. Bucky Harris quoted by Bill Dooly, "Bucky Harris Recalls High Spots in Life," *Philadelphia Record*: January 11, 1934.

18. "Boley, Baltimore Star, Comes Here," Philadelphia Public Ledger: October 16, 1926.

19. G. Edward White, *Creating the National Pastime: Baseball Transforms Itself, 1903-1953* (Princeton: Princeton University Press, 1996), 349–50.

20. *Scranton Republic*: July 10, 1911.

21. Butash, "Diogenes, Your Search Is Over!" 9.

22. Jack Bolton, "Fanned Babe Ruth to Start Major League Career," *The Sporting News*: June 7, 1929.

23. Kent Lindeman, "Mathewson Inducted to Baseball Hall of Fame in 1939," *Bucknellian* (April 21, 1989): 10; and Robinson, *Matty*, 19.

24. Mathewson quoted in "Mathewson Starting His Thirteenth Season with Giants Tells of His Early Trials That Beset His Advent in Baseball," *New York Evening Telegram*: April 2, 1912.

25. Robinson, *Matty*, 16–17.

26. Christy Mathewson to Bill?, August 10, 1899. Keystone College Archives.

27. Mathewson, "Mathewson Tells of Early Trials," (1915) Sherman Oaks, CA: Mathewson Foundation, 1997.

28. Sullivan, *Minors*, ix–x, 67–71.

29. John McCormick, "Baseball Memories," *Scranton/Wilkes-Barre Red Barons 1990 Scorecard and Magazine*, 97.

30. Pete Gray interview, Nanticoke, PA: August 10, 1994.

31. Mooney, "Pro Baseball Hit Wilkes-Barre."

32. McCormick, "Baseball Memories," 98. Scranton inherited the Red Sox farm club from Hazleton, which briefly hosted a Class D club.

33. Petula, *History of Scranton Baseball*, 27. Beginning in 1934 the Eastern League instituted a split schedule. At the end of the season, the winner of the first half played the winner of the second half in a seven-game series. The winner of that series became the league champion.

34. *Ibid.*, 27.

35. *Ibid.*, 31, 49.

36. Harry Dorish interview, Kingston, PA: December 30, 1999.

37. Joe Ostrowski interview, West Wyoming, PA: January 10, 2000.

38. *Ibid.*

39. Ken Buntz, "Coming Around Again," *Scranton/Wilkes-Barre Red Barons 1989 Scorecard and Magazine*, 7.

40. McCormick, "Baseball Memories," 100.

41. Thomas Moran quoted in Buntz, "Coming Around Again," 6.

42. Buntz, "Coming Around Again," 6; and McCormick, "Baseball Memories," 99.

43. *Wilkes-Barre Record*: September 1, 1948; and *The Scrantonian*: August 20, 1948.

44. Sullivan, *Minors*, x, 231–256.

45. Bob Duliba interview, West Pittston, PA: May 23, 1999.

46. "Duliba Player File," National Baseball Library, Cooperstown, NY.

47. Jon Carroll, "Hero Worship: Bilko's Army," *Beckett's Baseball Card Monthly* (April 1989): 14; and Jerry Izenberg, "Bilko Never Saw the Promised Land," *New York Post*: March 9, 1978.

48. Steve Bilko quoted in Rube Samuelson, "Time Running Out, Bilko Counts on Chance by Draft," *The Sporting News*: September 4, 1957.

49. *Rochester* (NY) *Democrat*: March 8, 1978.

50. Stan Pawloski interview, Philadelphia, PA: June 16, 1999.

51. "Meet the Indians," *Reading Times*: April 4, 1952; and "Four Reading Players Named on Eastern Manager's Team," *Reading Times*: July 1, 1952.

52. Gil Sweeney, "Still on His Feet, Stan Pawloski," *Indianapolis Star*: June 10, 1955.

53. Pawloski interview.

54. Sue Chylak quoted in Bob Krawczeniuk, "Nestor Chylak Jr. to Become Eighth Umpire in Hall of Fame," *Scranton Sunday Times*: July 25, 1999.

55. *Ibid.*

56. Mark Simon, "You're In! Induction Has Umpire's Son Beaming," *Scranton Times*: August 5, 1999.

57. Joe Paparella quoted in Chic Feldman, "Joe Paparella Awaits Silver Season," *Scrantonian*: February 4, 1962.

58. *Ibid.*

59. Buntz, "Coming Around Again," 7.

60. Mooney, "Pro Ball Hit Wilkes-Barre."

4. Serving Uncle Sam

1. David Q. Voigt, *American Baseball: From the Commissioners to Continental Expansion* (3 vols., University Park, PA: Penn State Press, 1983), II: 120.

2. *The Sporting News*: August 16, 23, 30, 1917.

3. Voigt, *American Baseball*, II: 121.

4. *Ibid.*, 122–23; and Harrington E. Crissey, Jr., "Baseball and the Armed Services," in *Total Baseball*, John Thorn and Peter Palmer, eds. (New York: Warner, 1989), 616.

5. Jerry Janowski, "Gazella Gave His Best at Lafayette and with the Yankees," *Mid-Valley News* (Lehighton, PA): February 3, 1994.

6. Robinson, *Matty*, 190–91.

7. *Ibid.*, 191. Other baseball notables who served the Chemical Warfare Service were Branch Rickey, the 38-year-old president of the St. Louis Cardinals and Ty Cobb, the 32-year-old star outfielder of the Detroit Tigers.

8. Robinson, *Matty*, 192–94.

9. Judge Kenesaw Mountain Landis quoted in Bill Gilbert, *They Also Served: Baseball and the Homefront, 1941–1945* (New York: Crown Publishers, 1992), 41.

10. President Franklin D. Roosevelt quoted in *Ibid.*, 42.

11. William Mead, *Baseball Goes to War* (Washington, D.C.: Farragut, 1985), 87–88.

12. Sheldon Spear, *Wyoming Valley Revisited* (Shavertown, PA: Jemags & Co., 1994), 210–11.

13. Bill Gutman, *The Golden Age of Baseball 1941–1963* (New York: Gallery Books, 1989), 22.

14. Ostrowski interview: January 10, 2000.

15. Dorish interview: December 30, 1999.

16. Jack Seitzinger, "Nestor Chylak, Umpire Great, Dead at 59," *Scranton Tribune*: February 18, 1982.

17. Chic Feldman, "Paparella, American League Senior Umpire," *Scrantonian*: January 20, 1963.

18. Gray interview: June 19, 1990.

19. *The Sporting News*: September 21, 1944.

20. *Washington Post*: May 31, 1945.

21. Gray quoted in *Toronto Star Weekly*: March 24, 1945.

22. See *Time Magazine*: June 12, 1944; *Saturday Evening Post*: July 10, 1944; *Sporting News*: August 17, 31 and September 14, 1944.

23. Gray interview: March 6, 1991.

24. Crissey, "Baseball and the Armed Services," 620–21.

25. Pawloski interview: June 16, 1999.

26. Bob Kurland, "Stan's Booming Bat, Educated Glove Leading Him To Cleveland," *Fort Lee Traveller*: June 4, 1954; See also "Lee's Pawloski May Be Cure For Indians' Second Base Ills," *Fort Lee Traveller*: June 17, 1953; and "Pawloski's Hit in 11th Brings Travellers 15th Straight Victory," *Fort Lee Traveller*: July 7, 1953.

27. Pawloski interview: June 16, 1999.

28. Duliba interview: May 23, 1999.

5. *Cooperstown Bound*

1. In 1999, *The Sporting News,* which has covered baseball since 1886, ranked the 100 best players of the century from a roster of about 15,000. A selection committee made up of 12 *TSN* editors was asked to choose the all-time 100 best players after a five-stage, select/ranking process. The final ranking were admittedly subjective and open to debate, but represent the collective finding of TSN, which has analyzed baseball history for more than a century. Mathewson finished 7th

all-time in that ranking, and Walsh, 82nd. (See Ron Smith, *The Sporting News Selects Baseball's Greatest Players: A Celebration of the 20th Century's Best* [St. Louis: The Sporting News, 1999]). Also in 1999, Major League Baseball distributed more than 35 million ballots to fans throughout North America to identify the top 100 players of the 20th century. Of that number, only 30 were named by Major League Baseball to an All-Century Team. Mathewson was selected one of only nine pitchers on that team. (See Mark Vancil & Peter Hirst. *All Century Team* [Chicago: Rare Air Books, 1999]).

2. National Baseball Hall of Fame, *2000 Yearbook* (Cooperstown, NY: National Baseball Hall of Fame, 2000), 54.

3. Harold Seymour, *Baseball: The Early Years* (New York: Oxford University, 1989, paperback edition), 104–116; and G. Edward White, *Creating the National Pastime: Baseball Transforms Itself, 1903–1953* (Princeton: Princeton University, 1996), 50–83.

4. Seymour, *Early Years*, 283–87.

5. Fullerton, "At-a-Boy!" 50.

6. *Ibid.*, 51.

7. Miller Huggins quoted in *ibid.*, 53.

8. Joseph X. Flannery, "Dohertys of Scranton Will See Cornell Honor Famous Kin," *Scranton Times*: September 10, 1998.

9. Jim Langford, "Hughie Jennings," in *The Ballplayers: Baseball's Ultimate Biographical Reference*, ed. Mike Shatzkin (New York: William Morrow, 1990), 524.

10. *Ibid.*

11. Sam Crawford quoted in Lawrence S. Ritter, *The Glory of Their Times: The Story of the Early Days of Baseball Told by the Men Who Played It* (New York: Vintage Books, 1985), 51.

12. Fullerton, "At-a-Boy!" 53.

13. Charles C. Alexander, *Ty Cobb* (New York: Oxford University, 1985), 50–53; and Richard Bak, *Ty Cobb: His Tumultuous Life and Times* (Dallas, TX: Taylor Publishing Company, 1994), 30.

14. Jennings quoted in *Detroit Free Press*: March 17, 1907.

15. Ty Cobb with Al Stump, *My Life in Baseball: The True Record* (1961; reprint, Lincoln: University of Nebraska Press, 1993), 192–196.

16. Bob Addie, "Harris Dies on 81st Birthday," *Washington Post*: November 10, 1977.

17. "Bucky Has Climbed to Dizzy Heights from Deep in a Coal Mine," *Washington Evening Star*: September 19, 1924.

18. Shirley Povich, "'Boy Wonder Led Senators to Only Title," *The Washington Post*: November 10, 1977.

19. "Senators Win in 12th,"*Washington Post*: October 20, 1924.

20. Jim Langford, "Bucky Harris," *Ballplayers*, 447.

21. Charles A. McCarthy, "'Boy Wonder Was Here 50 Years Ago," *Sunday Independent* (Wilkes-Barre, PA): September 22, 1974.

22. Langford, "Bucky Harris," 447.

23. *Ibid.*

24. See James A. Cox, *The Lively Ball: Baseball in the Roaring Twenties* (Alexandria, VA: Redefinition, 1989), 63–76. While cork was first added to the rubber

center of the baseball in 1909, batting averages did not begin to rocket until 1920 with the introduction of a much livelier ball. In fact, combined major league batting averages for 1920 were almost 30 points higher (from .248 to .276) than those of 1915. During the same period, earned run averages went up nearly a full point from 2.71 to 3.46.

25. See McGraw quoted in Robinson, *Matty*, 218; and Connie Mack, *My 66 Years in the Big Leagues* (Philadelphia: John C. Winston Company, 1950), 126.

26. John M. Harris, "'Pinhead' Christy Mathewson Was Unpopular and Unhappy Before McGraw Arrived," *National Pastime* (1997): 17–20.

27. Shatzkin, *Ballplayers*, 682.

28. Chief Meyers quoted in Ritter, *Glory of Their Times*, 176.

29. Chief Meyers quoted in Lowell Reidenbaugh, *Baseball's 25 Greatest Teams* (St. Louis: The Sporting News, 1988), 150.

30. Ring W. Lardner, "Matty," *The American Magazine* (August 1911): 26–29.

31. Ray Robinson, in his book, *Matty: An American Hero*, argues that "no player before his time — or after — ever captured the public fancy the way Mathewson did." A "watershed figure," the Giants pitcher "defined baseball with his brains, demeanor and attractive personality, plus his achievements on the field." He was, according to Robinson, "the first authentic sports hero." (See Robinson, *Matty*, 7–8).

32. Fred Snodgrass quoted in Ritter, *Glory of Their Times*, 96.

33. Chief Meyers quoted in Ritter, *Glory of Their Times*, 176.

34. Mathewson managed a great career despite having to adjust to a sometimes difficult schedule because of his refusal to pitch on a Sunday. Interestingly, whenever he pitched on a Saturday on short rest, with only two days between starts, or on a Monday on long rest with fours days between starts, his career record was 30-14 (.682)— higher than his .656 winning percentage in other, more regularly scheduled starts. At the same time, Mathewson was not forced to adjust that often since Sunday ball was legal only in Chicago, Cincinnati, and St. Louis during his career. (See Vancil & Hirdt, *All-Century Team*, 196).

35. Mathewson quoted in Lindeman, "Mathewson Inducted into Hall of Fame," 19.

36. Snyder quoted in Keisling, "Mathewson's Catcher."

37. Charles C. Alexander, *John McGraw* (New York: Penguin Books, 1989), 101–102; and *New York Times*: November 13, 1910.

38. Snodgrass quoted in Ritter, *Glory of Their Times*, 96.

39. Lloyd Lewis, "Christy Mathewson," in *My Greatest Day in Baseball*, ed. John P. Carmichael (New York: Grosset & Dunlap, 1945), 147–153.

40. John McGraw quoted in Robinson, *Matty*, 173–74.

41. Mathewson quoted in *Ibid.*, 175.

42. Ring Lardner quoted in *Ibid.*, 176.

43. See Smith, *Baseball's Greatest Players*, 22, and Shatzkin, *Ballplayers*, 681.

44. Smith, *Baseball's Greatest Players*, 178.

45. Sam Crawford quoted in Ritter, *Glory of Their Times*, 56.

46. Ed Walsh as told to Frank Monardo, "Pitching Only 30 Percent Now — Walsh," *The Sporting News*: January 9, 1957.

47. *Ibid.*

48. Richard C. Lindberg, "Ed Walsh," *Ballplayers*, 1137.

49. *Ibid.*

50. Ed Walsh as told to Francis J. Powers, *My Greatest Day in Baseball*, ed. John P. Carmichael (New York: Grosset & Dunlap, 1945), 236–40.

51. Mark Fitzhenry, "Pitching Machine Rode Durability to Cooperstown," *Times Leader* (Wilkes-Barre, PA): December 19, 1999.

52. Ed Walsh quoted in *Ibid.*

53. Smith, *Baseball's Greatest Players*, 178.

54. After Cleveland shortstop Ray Chapman was struck in the temple and killed by a pitch from Yankee submariner Carl Mays on August 16, 1920, major league baseball outlawed all trick pitches, including the spitball. Only a handful of pitchers, who had already established themselves as spitballers, were permitted to continue throwing the pitch, including Coveleski. (See Mike Sowell, *The Pitch That Killed: Carl Mays, Ray Chapman and the Pennant Race of 1920* [New York: Macmillan, 1991]).

55. Coveleski interview, National Baseball Hall of Fame.

56. "He Was Known as Covey," *Stanley Coveleski Regional Stadium 1987 Souvenir Program*, 11.

57. Coveleski interview.

58. *Ibid.*

59. A. D. Sueshdorf, "Stan Coveleski," *Ballplayers*, 228–29.

60. Coveleski interview.

61. Coveleski quoted in Ritter, *Glory of Their Times*, 117–18.

62. Sueshdorf, "Stan Coveleski, 229.

63. Mark Simon, "You're In! Induction Has Ump's Son Beaming," *Scranton Times*: August 5, 1999.

64. Chylak quoted in Borys Krawczeniuk, "Brooks Says Nestor Was the Best," *Scranton Sunday Times*: July 25, 1999.

65. Brooks Robinson quoted in *Ibid.*

66. Yogi Berra quoted in "Friends Recall Times Shared with Nestor," *Scranton Sunday Times*: July 25, 1999.

67. Rich Marrazzi, "Nestor Chylak," *Ballplayers*, 188.

68. "Nestor Chylak, Umpire Great, Is Dead at 59," *Scranton Tribune*: February 18, 1982.

69. Bob Krawczeniuk, "Nestor Chylak Jr., to Become Eighth Umpire in Hall of Fame," *Scranton Sunday Times*: July 25, 1999.

70. "Friends Recall Times Shared with Nestor," *Scranton Sunday Times*: July 25, 1999.

71. See Bill James, *The Politics of Glory: How Baseball's Hall of Fame Really Works* (New York: Macmillan, 1994).

6. Living the Dream

1. G. Edward White, *Creating the National Pastime: Baseball Transforms Itself, 1903–1953* (Princeton: Princeton University Press, 1996), 4.

2. *Ibid.*, 323–24.

3. *Ibid.*, 57–58, 84–126.

4. Van Rose, "When a Home Run Champ Was the Hometown Hero," *Times Leader* (Wilkes-Barre, PA): September 21, 1998; and Jim Langford, "Buck Freeman," *Ballplayers*, 360.

5. *Washington Evening Star*: June 10, 1899.

6. Charles A. McCarthy, "Wilkes-Barre Homer King, 'Bucky' Freeman, Set Big League Mark in 1899," *Sunday Independent* (Wilkes-Barre, PA): April 18, 1976. For a comparison, the Philadelphia Phillies, notorious for being one of the cheapest clubs in the history of baseball, agreed to pay its star second baseman, Napoleon Lajoie, $2,400 for the 1901 season before he jumped to the rival American League Athletics. (See Philadelphia Ball Club, Ltd. v. Lajoie, 202 Pa at 212-13 Pennsylvania Supreme Court Records, 1902).

7. See Miller and Sharpless, *Kingdom of Coal*, 242. Coal miners' wages are based on those prior to 1902 when the United Mine Workers was able to unionize labor in the coal industry and went out on strike for better pay and working conditions. That strike resulted in a 10 percent pay increase as well as better working conditions for the miners. Still, the improved wages did not come close to those star ballplayers were earning at the time.

8. Butash, "Diogenes, Your Search Is Over!" 9–10.

9. See David M. Jordan, *The Athletics of Philadelphia: Connie Mack's White Elephants* (Jefferson, NC: McFarland, 1999), 69–70.

10. Connie Mack, *My 66 Years in the Big Leagues* (Philadelphia: John C. Winston, 1950), 35–36.

11. Lee Allen, "Eddie Murphy Rolls Back the Years," *The Sporting News*: 1969.

12. Rob Neyer and Eddie Epstein, *Baseball Dynasties* (New York: W. W. Norton & Co., 2000), 48.

13. For salary figures, see Harvey Frommer, *Shoeless Joe and Ragtime Baseball* (Dallas, TX: Taylor Publishing, 1992), 64; and Irving M. Stein, *The Ginger Kid: The Buck Weaver Story* (Dubuque, IA: Elysian Fields, 1992), 126.

14. Frommer, *Shoeless Joe*, 64.

15. For the most comprehensive history of the Black Sox scandal see Eliot Asinof, *Eight Men Out: The Black Sox Scandal and the 1919 World Series* (New York: Henry Holt, 1963).

16. *Scranton Tribune*: February 22, 1969. Pitcher Dickie Kerr, another honest member of the Black Sox, dubbed Murphy the "Honest hero of the Series," even though he went hitless in two plate appearances.

17. See Murphy quoted in Allen, "Eddie Murphy Rolls Back the Years," and quoted in Stein, *Ginger Kid*, 239.

18. Eddie Murphy Jr. interview, Dunmore, PA: December 10, 2000; and Butash, "Diogenes, Your Search Is Over!" 10.

19. A. D. Sueshdorf, "Jake Daubert," *Ballplayers*, 252. See Bill James, *The Politics of Glory: How Baseball's Hall of Fame Really Works* (New York: Macmillan, 1994), 283. James identifies Daubert as one of the most outstanding first basemen of his era and one who deserves a bronze plaque in Cooperstown.

20. John W. Smith, "In 1913, Jake Daubert Struck Blow for Ballplayers' Rights," *The Reading Eagle*: August 10, 1994; and "Coal Mine to Major League Batting Champion," *Schuylkill Haven Call*: July 10, 1997.

21. Daubert quoted in *Baseball Magazine* (February 1914): 12.

22. Seymour, *Baseball: Golden Age*, 220, 253.

23. John H. Gruber, "Coal Digger When a Youth, Now He's a Batting Champion," *Philadelphia Public Ledger*: March 7, 1915.

24. Daubert to August Herrmann, November 9, 1921. National Baseball Hall of Fame Library.

25. Sueshdorf, "Jake Daubert," *Ballplayers*, 252.

26. Voigt, "History of Major League Baseball," 19. By 1929 Americans were annually spending $4.9 billion for recreational entertainment. Voigt points out that much of that money was spent on movies, radios and automobiles, but baseball was also attracting millions of fans.

27. For the most complete biography of Babe Ruth see Robert W. Creamer, *BABE: The Legend Comes to Life* (New York: Simon and Schuster, 1974).

28. Jerry Janowski, "Gazella Gave His Best at Lafayette and with the Yankees," *Mid-Valley News*: February 3, 1994.

29. *New York Times*: October 8, 1926.

30. Leo Trachtenberg, *The Wonder Team:The True Story of the Incomparable 1927 New York Yankees* (Bowling Green, OH: Popular Press, 1995), 71.

31. *New York Evening Journal*: April 1, 1927.

32. Trachtenberg, *The Wonder Team*, 71.

33. Shaute quoted in Jack Bolton, "Fanned Babe Ruth to Start Major League Career," *Sporting News*: June 7, 1929.

34. Shaute quoted in *Scrantonian*: March 7, 1970.

35. *Ibid.*

36. Shaute quoted in Chick Feldman, "Indians Paid Shaute $6,000 for Winning 20 Games in 1924," *Scrantonian*: December 25, 1966.

37. Wolf, *Baseball Encyclopedia*, 2196–97.

38. Shaute quoted in Feldman, "Indians Paid Shaute $6,000."

39. Wolff, *Baseball Encyclopedia*, 1304–05, 2645.

40. James, *Politics of Glory*, 111.

41. "O'Neill Quit Mines to Start Baseball Career," *Wilkes-Barre Record*: August 5, 1935.

42. Steve O'Neill quoted in Cy Kritzer, "O'Neill Always a 'Ball Player's Pilot," *Sporting News*: July 5, 1950.

43. Hughie Jennings quoted in *Ibid.*

44. Jack Kavanagh, "Steve O'Neill," *Ballplayers*, 828.

45. Robin Roberts quoted in Chick Feldman, "The Day O'Neill Cried," *Scrantonian*: January 28, 1962.

46. Jim Langford, "Jack Quinn," *Ballplayers*, 887.

47. Evans, "Jack Quinn: Stitching a Baseball Legend," 7–9.

48. Jack Quinn quoted in Walter S. Farquhar, "Sportitorial," *Pottsville Journal*: n.d.

49. *New York Times*: April 16, 1909. In fairness to Quinn, many years later in 1919 he did face Johnson in a scoreless tie. The game went 12 innings before it was called. Johnson did, in fact, consider this to be one of the greatest pitching duels he ever experienced. (See Henry W. Thomas, *Walter Johnson. Baseball's Big Train* [New York: Phenom Press, 1995], 355).

50. Quinn quoted in Farquhar, "Sportitorial."

51. *Wilkes-Barre Record*: December 22, 1933.

52. *New York Times*: October 13, 1929.

53. Jack Quinn quoted in Austen Lake, "Good Legs Vital to Good Pitching," *Philadelphia Public Ledger*: February 7, 1925; and Helen Bisset, "Mrs. Jack Quinn Tells of Husband's Success," *American Sports*: June 12, 1925.

54. Langford, "Quinn," 887.

55. Miller quoted in *Times Leader* (Wilkes-Barre, PA): December 31, 1962.

56. *Ibid.*

57. For more information on baseball during World War II see Bill Gilbert, *They Also Served: Baseball and the Home Front, 1941–1945* (New York: Crown, 1992); Richard Goldstein, *Spartan Seasons: How Baseball Survived the Second World War* (New York: Macmillan, 1980); Mead, *Baseball Goes to War*.

58. White, *Creating the National Pastime*, 321–24.

59. Gray's critics include Bill Gutman, *The Golden Age of Baseball, 1941–1963* (New York: Gallery Books, 1989), 30; Goldstein, *Spartan Seasons*, 208–10; Mead, *Baseball Goes to War*, 209; and Daniel Okrent and Harris Lewine, *The Ultimate Baseball Book* (Boston: Houghton-Mifflin, 1981), 221.

60. Gray quoted in *The Sporting News*: March 22, 1945.

61. Sewell quoted in ibid.

62. *Washington Post*: May 31, 1945.

63. *St. Louis Post-Dispatch*: May 21, 1945.

64. Pete Gray interview, Nanticoke, PA: March 6, 1991.

65. *Ibid.*

66. Wolf, *Baseball Encyclopedia*, 963.

67. Harry Dorish interview, Kingston, PA: December 30, 1999.

68. Wolff, *Baseball Encyclopedia*, 1793.

69. Dorish interview.

70. Joe Ostrowski interview, West Wyoming, PA: January 10, 2000.

71. Wolff, *Baseball Encyclopedia*, 2103.

72. Ostrowski interview.

73. Wolff, *Baseball Encyclopedia*, 2103.

74. Stan Pawloski interview, Philadelphia, PA: June 16, 1999.

75. Ibid.

76. Warner O. Rockford, "Steve Bilko," *Ballplayers*, 78.

77. Wolff, *Baseball Encyclopedia*, 683.

78. Bob Duliba interview, West Pittston, PA: May 23, 1999.

79. Wolff, *Baseball Encyclopedia*, 1800.

80. Duliba interview.

81. Wolff, *Baseball Encyclopedia*, 1800.

82. Chic Feldman, "Paparella Awaits Silver Season," *Scrantonian*: February 4, 1962.

83. Paparella quoted in *Ibid.*

84. Chic Feldman, "Paparella American League Senior Umpire," *Scrantonian*: January 20, 1963.

85. Paparella quoted in Feldman, "Paparella Awaits Silver Season."

86. Rich Marazzi, "Joe Paparella," *Ballplayers*, 843.

7. Quittin' Time

1. Miller and Sharpless, *Kingdom of Coal*, 323.

2. Robinson, *Matty*, 181.

3. *Ibid.* 196, 203–04, 210–11.

4. Mathewson quoted in *Ibid.*, 215.

5. Grantland Rice, "Tribute to Christy Mathewson," *New York Herald Tribune*: October 9, 1925.

6. Leo F. Gleason, "Matty," *The Philadelphia Inquirer*: October 28, 1925.

7. Robinson, *Matty*, 3–8, 217–25.

8. Eric Rolfe Greenberg, *The Celebrant* (Lincoln: University of Nebraska Press, 1983).

9. "Mathewson Collection in Acquired," *Keynotes: The Alumni Magazine of Keystone Junior College* (Autumn, 1967): 2; and Michael J. Rudolph, "Factoryville celebrates Christy Mathewson Day," *New Age Examiner*: August 13, 1996.

10. Kent Lindeman, "Mathewson Inducted into Baseball Hall of Fame in 1939," *Bucknellian* (April 21, 1989): 19.

11. Robinson, *Matty*, 216.

12. Jake Daubert to Butch Yoder of Shoemakersville, PA: September 2, 1924. National Baseball Library.

13. John W. Smith, "In 1913, Jake Daubert Struck a Blow for Ballplayers' Rights," *Reading Eagle*: August 10. 1994.

14. See *Wilkes-Barre Times Leader*: April 30, 1946 & May 18, 1948; *St. Louis Post-Dispatch*: May 18, 1948.

15. Gray interview: August 13, 1992.

16. See Joe Falls, "Once Upon a Time There Was a One-Armed Outfielder … in the Major Leagues," *Sport Magazine* (January 1973): 23–6, 86–7. Falls, a Detroit sportswriter, paid an unexpected visit to Gray in the fall of 1972 after being told by the former Brownie to "stay away." After convincing friends and relatives that his intentions were good, Falls was granted a two-hour interview by Gray, the first since he retired from professional baseball in 1949.

17. *New York Daily News*: April 14, 1986; *New York Post*: April 14, 1986.

18. William C. Kashatus, *One-Armed Wonder: Pete Gray, Wartime Baseball and the American Dream* (Jefferson, NC: McFarland & Company, 1995); see also Dave Kindred, "Coal Miner's Son," *The Sporting News 1995 Baseball Yearbook*, 159–60; and Joe Clark, "Wrote This One for You, Pete: One-Armed Major League Outfielder Author's Hero Since Age 6," *The Philadelphia Daily News*: May 2, 1995.

19. Evans, "Quinn," 21.

20. Jerry Izenberg, "Bilko Never Saw the Promised Land," *New York Post*: March 9, 1978.

21. Jon Carroll, "Hero Worship: Bilko's Army," *Beckett's Baseball Card Monthly* (April 1989): 14.

22. Interview with Steve Bilko Jr., Nanticoke, PA: November 30, 2000; and *Wilkes-Barre Times Leader*: March 8, 1978.

23. "Baseball Loses One of Its Best Loved and Most Loveable Sons," *Wilkes-Barre Record*: February 2, 1928.

24. "Jennings' Condition Critical," *Asheville Press*: April 7, 1927.

25. Fullerton, "At-a-Boy!" 53.

26. Joseph X. Flannery, "Doherty's of Scranton Will See Cornell Honor Famous Kin," *Scranton Times*: September 10, 1998.

27. Joe Reardon quoted in Chic Feldman, "The Day Steve O'Neill Cried," *Scrantonian*: January 28, 1962.

28. "Hundreds at Last Rites for Steve O'Neill; Cemetery Overlooks His Old Playing Field," *Scranton Times*: January 30, 1962.

29. Shirley Povich, "'Boy Wonder' Led Senators to Only Title," *Washington Post*: November 10, 1977.

30. "Ex-Yankee Pilot Harris Dies on 81st Birthday," *New York Daily News*: November 10, 1977.

31. Bob Addie, "Harris Dies on 81st Birthday," *Washington Post*: November 10, 1977.

32. *Ibid.*

33. *Ibid.*

34. Fitzhenry, "Pitching Machine Rode Durability to Cooperstown."

35. McCarthy, "Wilkes-Barre Homer King."

36. "Joe Boley Turns to Managing," *Wilkes-Barre Record*: April 4, 1935.

37. Trachtenberg, *Wonder Team*, 157–58.

38. *Scrantonian*: March 7, 1970.

39. Butash, "Diogenes," 11.

40. "He Was Known as 'Covey'," *Stanley Coveleski Regional Stadium 1987 Souvenir Program*, 11.

41. Bob Chylak interview, Newtown, PA: December 11, 2000.

42. Ostrowski interview.

43. Duliba interview.

44. Pawloski interview.

45. Seitzinger, "Nestor Chylak Dead at 59"; and Feldman, "Paparella Awaits Silver Season."

46. Pawloski interview.

Selected Bibliography

Bodnar, John. *Anthracite People: Families, Unions, and Work, 1900–1940.* Harrisburg: Pennsylvania Historical and Museum Commission, 1983.

Brown, John. "Hugh Jennings: The Live Wire of Modern Baseball," *Baseball Magazine* (July 1910): 35–39.

Carmichael, John P., ed. *My Greatest Day in Baseball.* New York: Grossett & Dunlap, 1945.

Carroll, Jon. "Hero Worship: Bilko's Army," *Beckett's Baseball Card Monthly* (April 1989): 14.

Chapman, John C. "How I Discovered Hughie Jennings," *Baseball Magazine* (July 1910): 25–26.

Cox, James A. *The Lively Ball: Baseball in the Roaring Twenties.* Alexandria, VA: Redefinition, Inc., 1989.

Evans, John W. "Jack Quinn: Stitching a Baseball Legend" (Unpublished paper delivered at American Catholic Historical Association Conference, April 1997)

Fullerton, Hugh. "At-a-Boy! How Hughie Jennings Fought His Way from the Mine Pits to the Pinnacle of Baseball Glory," *Liberty Magazine* (April 14, 1928): 49–53.

Gruber, John H. "Jake Daubert — Coal Digger When a Youth, Now He's a Batting Champion," *Philadelphia Public Ledger*: March 7, 1915.

Kashatus, William C. *One-Armed Wonder: Pete Gray, Wartime Baseball and the American Dream.* Jefferson, NC: McFarland, 1995.

Lardner, Ring W. "Matty," *American Magazine* (August 1911): 26–29.

Mathewson, Christy. *How I Came to Be a Big League Pitcher (1912)*. Sherman Oaks, CA: Mathewson Foundation, 1997.

McCarthy, Charles A. "Wilkes-Barre Homer King, 'Bucky' Freeman, Set Big League Mark in 1899," *Sunday Independent* (Wilkes-Barre, PA): April 18, 1976.

Miller, Donald L. and Richard E. Sharpless. *The Kingdom of Coal: Work, Enterprise, and Ethnic Communities in the Mine Fields*. Philadelphia: University of Pennsylvania, 1985.

New York Post: 1978–1989

New York Times: 1912–1978.

Petula, Nicolas E. *A History of Scranton Professional Baseball, 1865–1953*. Scranton, PA, 1989.

Philadelphia Inquirer: 1920–1950.

Philadelphia Public Ledger : 1915–1925.

Ralph, John J., ed. *The National Baseball Hall of Fame and Museum 2000 Yearbook*. Cooperstown, NY: National Baseball Hall of Fame, 2000.

Ritter, Lawrence S. *The Glory of Their Times: The Story of the Early Days of Baseball Told by the Men Who Played It*. New York: Vintage, 1985.

Robinson, Ray. *Matty: An American Hero*. New York: Oxford University Press, 1993.

Scranton (PA)*Times* : 1962–1999.

Scranton/Wilkes-Barre Red Barons Yearbooks: 1989–1999.

Scrantonian (Scranton, PA): 1969 –1970.

Seymour, Harold. *Baseball: The Golden Age*. New York: Oxford University Press, 1971.

Shatzkin, Mike, ed. *The Ballplayers: Baseball's Ultimate Biographical Reference*. New York: William Morrow, 1990.

Sporting News (St. Louis, Missouri): 1929–1967.

Times Leader (Wilkes-Barre, PA): 1978–1999.

Walsh, Ed. "The Advantage of Being Hard Headed," *Baseball Magazine* (April 1918): 459, 501.

White, Edward G. *Creating the National Pastime: Baseball Transforms Itself, 1903–1953*. Princeton: Princeton University, 1996.

Wilkes-Barre Record: 1928–1950

Wolff, Rick, ed. *The Baseball Encyclopedia*. New York: Macmillan, 1990.

Index